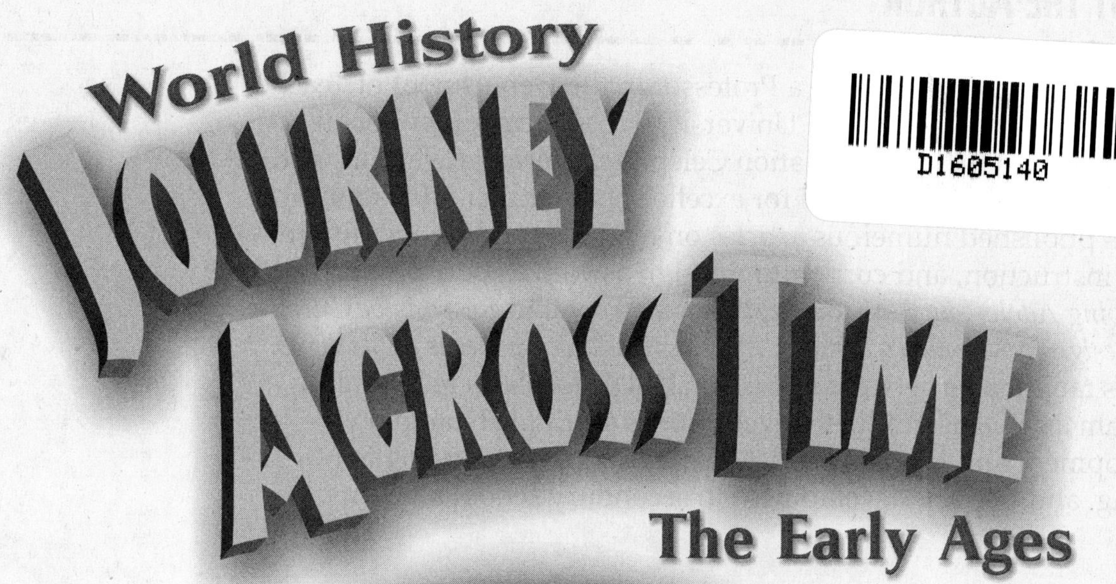

Active Reading Note-Taking Guide

Student Workbook

Douglas Fisher, Ph.D.
San Diego State University

New York, New York Columbus, Ohio Chicago, Illinois

About the Author

Douglas Fisher, Ph.D., is a Professor in the Department of Teacher Education at San Diego State University. He is the recipient of an International Reading Association Celebrate Literacy Award as well as a Christa McAuliffe award for excellence in teacher education. He has published numerous articles on reading and literacy, differentiated instruction, and curriculum design as well as books, such as *Improving Adolescent Literacy: Strategies at Work* and *Responsive Curriculum Design in Secondary Schools: Meeting the Diverse Needs of Students.* He has taught a variety of courses in SDSU's teacher-credentialing program as well as graduate-level courses on English language development and literacy. He has also taught classes in English, writing, and literacy development to secondary school students.

The McGraw·Hill Companies

Send all inquiries to:
Glencoe/McGraw-Hill
8787 Orion Place
Columbus, Ohio 43240-4027

ISBN: 978-0-07-878926-7
MHID: 0-07-878926-5

Printed in the United States of America.

7 8 9 10 MAL 12 11

Table of Contents

Table of Contents

Table of Contents

To the Student

Dear Social Studies Student,

Can you believe it? The start of another school year is upon you. How exciting to be learning about different cultures, historical events, and unique places in your social studies class! I believe that this* Active Reading Note-Taking Guide *will help you as you learn about your community, nation, and world.

Note-Taking and Student Success

Did you know that the ability to take notes helps you become a better student? Research suggests that good notes help you become more successful on tests because the act of taking notes helps you remember and understand content. This *Active Reading Note-Taking Guide* is a tool that you can use to achieve this goal. I'd like to share some of the features of this *Active Reading Note-Taking Guide* with you before you begin your studies.

The Cornell Note-Taking System

First, you will notice that the pages in the *Active Reading Note-Taking Guide* are arranged in two columns, which will help you organize your thinking. This two-column design is based on the **Cornell Note-Taking System**, developed at Cornell University. The column on the left side of the page highlights the main ideas and vocabulary of the lesson. This column will help you find information and locate the references in your textbook quickly. You can also use this column to sketch drawings that further help you visually remember the lesson's information. In the column on the right side of the page, you will write detailed notes about the main ideas and vocabulary. The notes you take in this column will help you focus on the important information in the lesson. As you become more comfortable using the **Cornell Note-Taking System**, you will see that it is an important tool that helps you organize information.

The Importance of Graphic Organizers

Second, there are many graphic organizers in this *Active Reading Note-Taking Guide*. Graphic organizers allow you to see the lesson's important information in a visual format. In addition, graphic organizers help you understand and summarize information, as well as remember the content.

Research-Based Vocabulary Development

Third, you will notice that vocabulary is introduced and practiced throughout the *Active Reading Note-Taking Guide*. When you know the meaning of the words used to discuss information, you are able to understand that information better. Also, you are more likely to be successful in school when you have vocabulary knowledge. When researchers study successful students, they find that as students acquire vocabulary knowledge, their ability to learn improves. The *Active Reading Note-Taking*

To the Student

Guide focuses on learning words that are very specific to understanding the content of your textbook. It also highlights general academic words that you need to know so that you can understand any textbook. Learning new vocabulary words will help you succeed in school.

Writing Prompts and Note-Taking

Finally, there are a number of writing exercises included in this *Active Reading Note-Taking Guide*. Did you know that writing helps you to think more clearly? It's true. Writing is a useful tool that helps you know if you understand the information in your textbook. It helps you assess what you have learned.

You will see that many of the writing exercises require you to practice the skills of good readers. Good readers *make connections* between their lives and the text and *predict* what will happen next in the reading. They *question* the information and the author of the text, *clarify* information and ideas, and *visualize* what the text is saying. Good readers also *summarize* the information that is presented and *make inferences* or *draw conclusions* about the facts and ideas.

I wish you well as you begin another school year. This *Active Reading Note-Taking Guide* is designed to help you understand the information in your social studies class. The guide will be a valuable tool that will also provide you with skills you can use throughout your life.

I hope you have a successful school year.

Sincerely,

Douglas Fisher

Chapter 1, Section 1
Early Humans
(Pages 8–15)

Main Idea

Setting a Purpose for Reading Think about these questions as you read:

- How did Paleolithic people adapt to their environment and use tools to help them survive?
- How did life change for people during the Neolithic Age?

Reading Strategy

As you read pages 9–15 in your textbook, complete this graphic organizer by filling in the causes and effects that explain how early humans adapted to their environment.

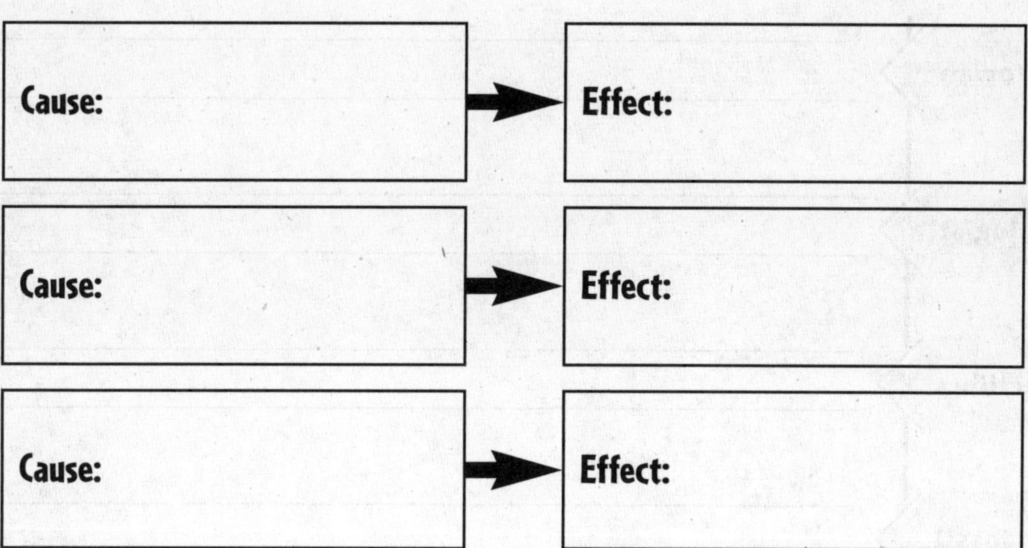

Early Humans *(pages 9–11)*

Visualizing

What would it be like to live in the Stone Age? As you read, list words and phrases that help you picture the life of early humans. Then write a paragraph describing a day in your life as a Paleolithic man or woman.

Terms To Know

Define or describe the following terms from this lesson.

historian

archaeologist

artifact

fossil

anthropologist

nomad

technology

Academic Vocabulary

Define these academic vocabulary words from this lesson.

period

task

Sum It Up

How are fossils and artifacts different?

Neolithic Times *(pages 13–15)*

Inferring

Why do some historians consider the farming revolution the most important event in human history? As you read, look for hints or ideas that support this idea. Record the hints you find in the web below.

The Farming Revolution

Terms To Know

Define or describe the following terms from this lesson.

domesticate

specialization

Places To Locate

Briefly describe the following place.

Jericho

Academic Vocabulary

Define these academic vocabulary words from this lesson.

revolution

affect

Sum It Up

How did the Paleolithic and Neolithic Ages differ?

Now that you have read the section, write the answers to the questions that were included in* Setting a Purpose for Reading *at the beginning of the lesson.

How did Paleolithic people adapt to their environment and use tools to help them survive?

How did life change for people during the Neolithic Age?

Chapter 1, Section 2
Mesopotamian Civilization

(Pages 16–23)

Main Idea

Setting a Purpose for Reading Think about these questions as you read:

- Why did civilization in Mesopotamia begin in the valleys of the Tigris and Euphrates Rivers?
- How did the Sumerians contribute to later peoples?
- Why did the Sumerian city-states lose power?

Reading Strategy

As you read pages 17–23 in your textbook, complete this diagram to show how the first empire in Mesopotamia came about.

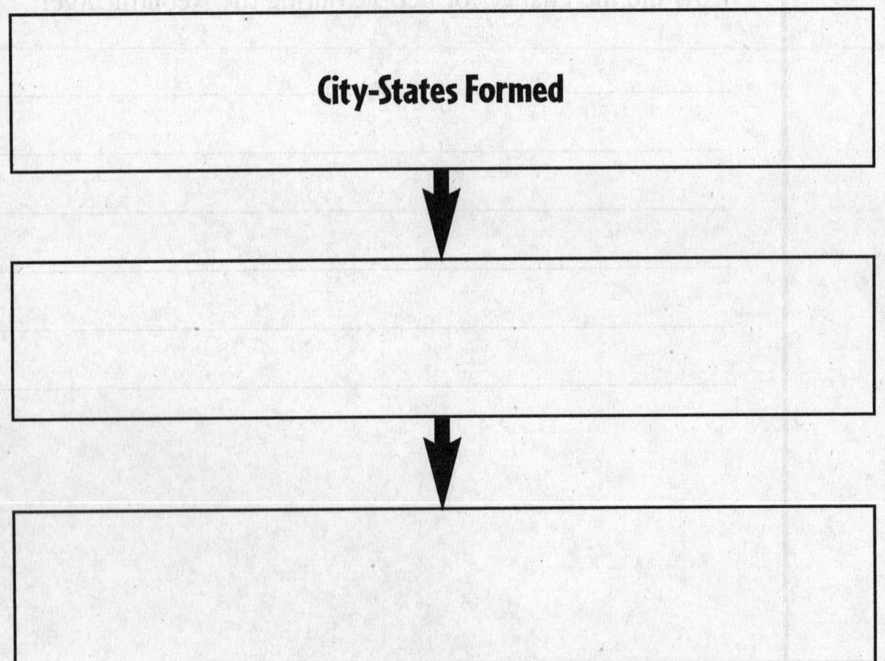

Mesopotamia's Civilization *(pages 17–20)*

Outlining ***Complete this outline as you read.***

I. Why Were River Valleys Important?

A. ______________________

B. ______________________

II. The Rise of Sumer

A. ______________________

B. ______________________

III. What Were City-States?

A. ______________________

B. ______________________

IV. Gods and Rulers

A. ______________________

B. ______________________

V. What Was Life Like in Sumer?

A. ______________________

B. ______________________

Terms To Know ***Define or describe the following terms from this lesson.***

civilization ______________________

irrigation ______________________

city-state

artisan

Places To Locate

Briefly describe the following places.

Mesopotamia

Tigris River

Euphrates River

Sumer

Academic Vocabulary

Define these academic vocabulary words from this lesson.

complex

assemble

Sum It Up ***How did Mesopotamians control the flow of the Tigris and Euphrates Rivers?***

A Skilled People *(pages 20–21)*

Drawing Conclusions ***As you read, write three details about the Sumerians. Then write a general statement on the basis of these details.***

1.

2.

3.

General Statement

Terms To Know

Define or describe the following terms from this lesson.

cuneiform

scribe

Academic Vocabulary

Define these academic vocabulary words from this lesson.

consist

create

Terms To Review

Use each of these terms that you studied earlier in a sentence that reflects the term's meaning.

archaeologist
(Chapter 1, Section 1)

technology
(Chapter 1, Section 1)

Sum It Up *What kind of written language did the Sumerians use?*

____

____

____

____

Sargon and Hammurabi *(page 23)*

Summarizing *As you read, complete the following sentences. Doing so will help you summarize the section.*

1. Sumeria was conquered by the ____________. Their king, ____________, set up the world's first ____________.

2. The Babylonian king ____________ is best known for his collection of ____________. While some of his laws seem cruel, they were an important step toward a fair system of ____________.

Terms To Know *Define or describe the following term from this lesson.*

empire ____

____

Places To Locate *Briefly describe the following place.*

Babylon ____

____

People To Meet

Explain why each of these people is important.

Sargon

Hammurabi

Academic Vocabulary

Define these academic vocabulary words from this lesson.

conflict

code

Sum It Up

Why was Sargon's empire important?

Now that you have read the section, write the answers to the questions that were included in* Setting a Purpose for Reading *at the beginning of the lesson.

Why did civilization in Mesopotamia begin in the valleys of the Tigris and Euphrates Rivers?

How did the Sumerians contribute to later peoples?

Why did the Sumerian city-states lose power?

Chapter 1, Section 3
The First Empires

(Pages 26–30)

Main Idea

Setting a Purpose for Reading Think about these questions as you read:

- How did Assyria build its vast empire?
- What major contributions did the Chaldean Empire make?

Reading Strategy

As you read pages 27–30 in your textbook, complete this diagram listing the similarities and differences between the Assyrian and Chaldean Empires.

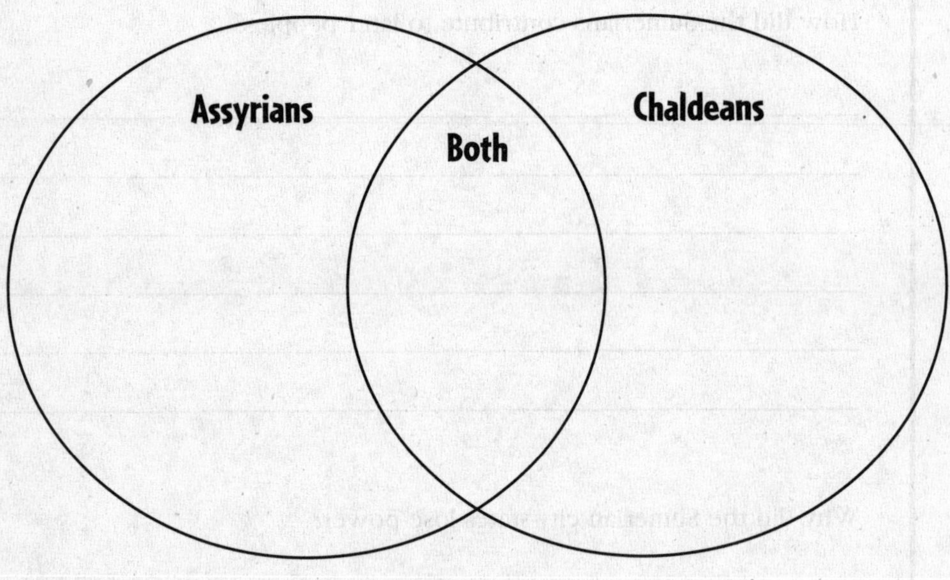

The Assyrians *(pages 27–28)*

Questioning

As you read, write three questions about the main ideas presented in this passage. After you have finished reading, write the answers to these questions.

1. ______________________________

____

____

2. ______________________________

____

____

3. ______________________________

____

____

Terms To Know

Define or describe the following term from this lesson.

province ______________________________

____

Places To Locate

Briefly describe the following places.

Assyria ______________________________

____

Nineveh ______________________________

____

Persian Gulf ______________________________

____

Notes

Academic Vocabulary

Define these academic vocabulary words from this lesson.

founded

core

Sum It Up

Why were the Assyrian soldiers considered brutal and cruel?

The Chaldeans *(pages 29–30)*

Determining the Main Idea

As you read, write the main idea of the passage. Review your statement when you have finished reading and revise as needed.

Terms To Know

Define or describe the following terms from this lesson.

caravan

astronomer

Places To Locate

Briefly describe the following place.

Hanging Gardens

People To Meet

Explain why this person is important.

Nebuchadnezzar

Academic Vocabulary

Define these academic vocabulary words from this lesson.

interval

route

Sum It Up

What were the Hanging Gardens of Babylon?

Now that you have read the section, write the answers to the questions that were included in* Setting a Purpose for Reading *at the beginning of the lesson.

How did Assyria build its vast empire?

What major contributions did the Chaldean Empire make?

Chapter 2, Section 1
The Nile Valley

(Pages 38–46)

Main Idea

Setting a Purpose for Reading Think about these questions as you read:

- Why did the early Egyptians settle in the Nile River valley?
- What role did the Nile River valley play in the development of the Egyptian civilization?
- How was early Egyptian society divided?

Reading Strategy

As you read pages 39-42 in your textbook, complete this diagram to describe Egyptian irrigation systems.

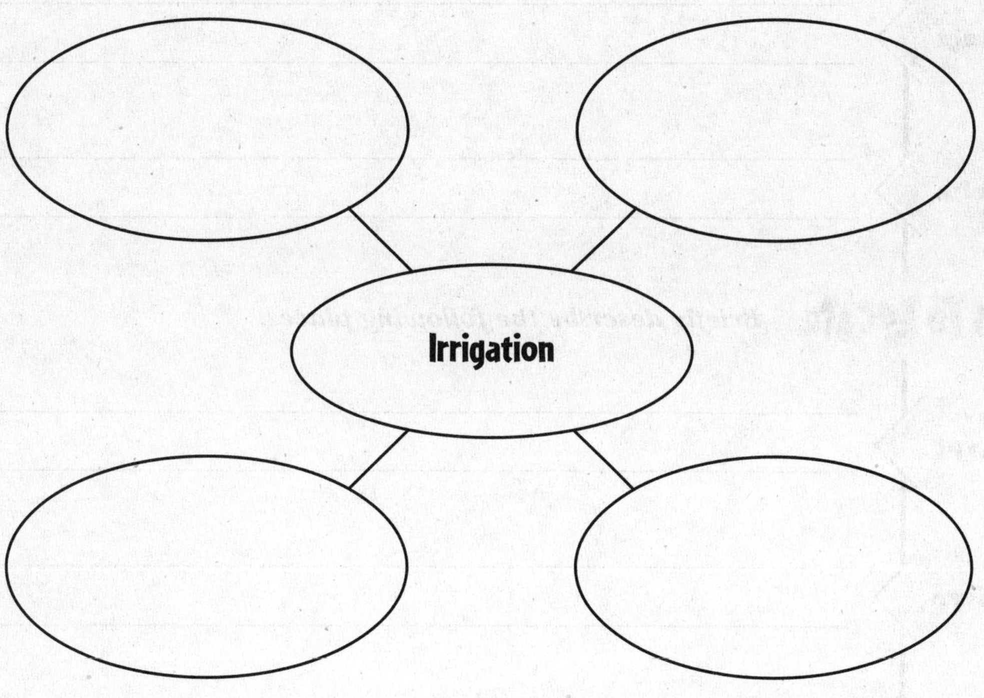

Settling the Nile *(pages 39–40)*

Determining the Main Idea

As you read, take notes describing the Nile and the area surrounding this great river. Use your notes to answer this question: How did the Nile and the surrounding area help protect Egypt?

Terms To Know

Define or describe the following terms from this lesson.

cataract

delta

Places To Locate

Briefly describe the following places.

Egypt

Nile River

Sahara

Academic Vocabulary

Define these academic vocabulary words from this lesson.

rely

feature

Terms To Review

Use each of these terms that you studied earlier in a sentence that reflects the term's meaning.

civilization
(Chapter 1, Section 2)

city-state
(Chapter 1, Section 2)

Sum It Up

What was Egypt's physical setting like?

The River People *(pages 41–42)*

Questioning

As you read, write three questions about the main ideas presented in the passage. After you have finished reading, write the answers to these questions.

1.

Key Points | Notes

2.

3.

Terms To Know

Define or describe the following terms from this lesson.

papyrus

hieroglyphics

Academic Vocabulary

Define these academic vocabulary words from this lesson.

secure

technology

Terms To Review

Use each of these terms, that you studied earlier, in a sentence that reflects the term's meaning.

irrigation
(Chapter 1, Section 2)

technology
(Chapter 1, Section 1)

Sum It Up *What crops did ancient Egyptians grow?*

A United Egypt *(pages 43–44)*

Drawing Conclusions ***As you read, write three details about Narmer. Then write a general statement about Narmer's leadership on the basis of these details.***

1.

2.

3.

General Statement

Terms To Know ***Define or describe the following term from this lesson.***

dynasty

Key Points | Notes

People To Meet *Explain why this person is important.*

Narmer

____

____

Academic Vocabulary *Define this academic vocabulary word from this lesson.*

emerge

____

____

Sum It Up *What is a dynasty?*

____

____

____

____

Early Egyptian Life *(pages 45–46)*

Summarizing *As you read, complete the following sentences. Doing so will help you summarize the section.*

1. The ______________ was at the top of the early Egyptian social structure.

2. Egypt's upper class was made up of ______________.

3. Egypt's middle class included people who ______________.

4. ______________ made up the largest group of early Egyptians.

5. ______________ were at the bottom of the social structure in Egypt.

6. ______________ had more rights in Egypt than in most other early civilizations.

Academic Vocabulary

Define these academic vocabulary words from this lesson.

portion ______________________________

obtain ______________________________

Sum It Up

Who made up the largest group in Egyptian society?

____

Now that you have read the section, write the answers to the questions that were included in* Setting a Purpose for Reading *at the beginning of the lesson.

Why did the early Egyptians settle in the Nile River valley?

What role did the Nile River valley play in the development of the Egyptian civilization?

How was early Egyptian society divided?

Chapter 2, Section 2

Egypt's Old Kingdom

(Pages 47–52)

Main Idea

Setting a Purpose for Reading Think about these questions as you read:

- What were the main Egyptian beliefs about deities and the afterlife?
- Why did Egyptians build pyramids?

Reading Strategy

As you read pages 49–50 in your textbook, complete this graphic organizer to show the different religious beliefs in Egypt.

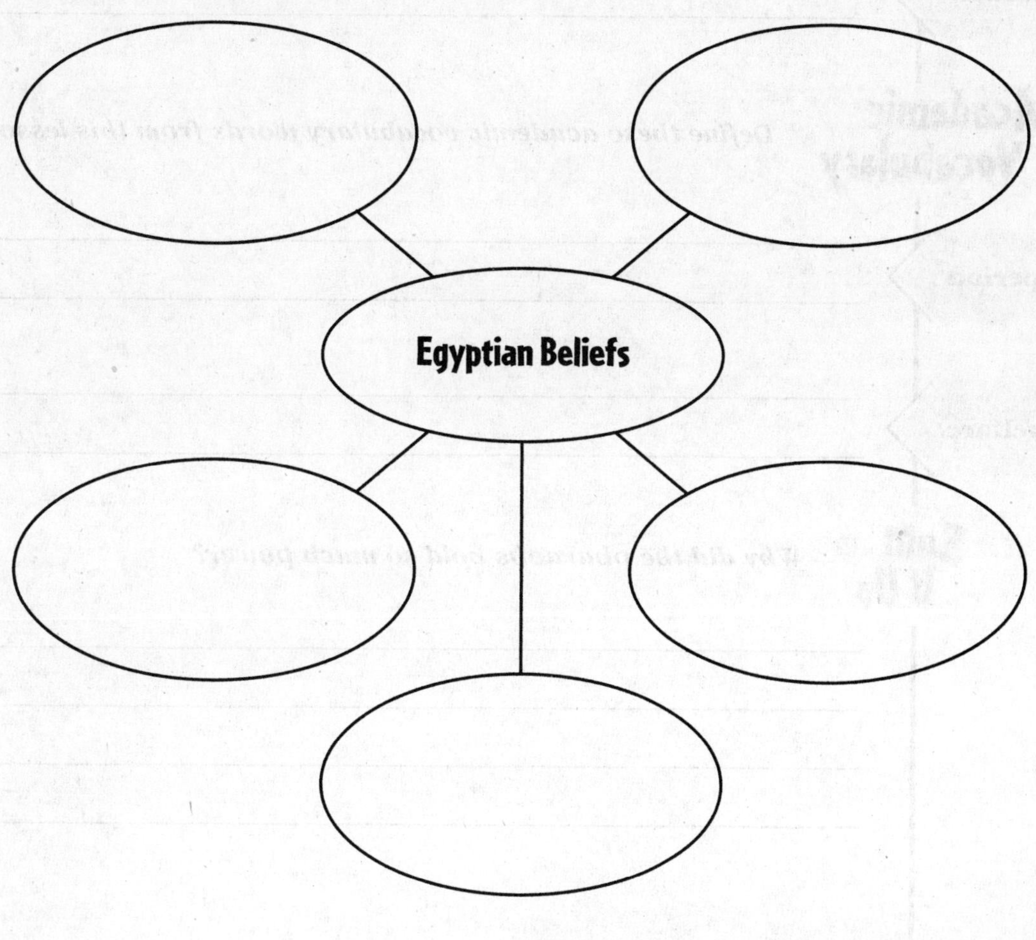

Old Kingdom Rulers *(page 48)*

Determining the Main Idea

As you read, write the main idea of the passage. Review your statement when you have finished reading and revise as needed.

Terms To Know

Define or describe the following term from this lesson.

pharaoh

Academic Vocabulary

Define these academic vocabulary words from this lesson.

period

welfare

Sum It Up

Why did the pharaohs hold so much power?

Egypt's Religion *(pages 49–50)*

Previewing

To preview this section, first skim the section. Then write a sentence or two explaining what you think you will be learning. After you have finished reading, revise your statements as necessary.

Terms To Know

Define or describe the following terms from this lesson.

deity

embalming

mummy

Academic Vocabulary

Define these academic vocabulary words from this lesson.

grant

medical

Sum It Up

Who were some of the main gods and goddesses of ancient Egypt?

The Pyramids *(pages 50–52)*

Inferring

Imagine standing at the foot of an ancient pyramid. What do these giant structures tell you about the Egyptian culture and people? As you read, take notes about the pyramids to help you answer this question.

Terms To Know

Define or describe the following term from this lesson.

pyramid

Places To Locate

Briefly describe the following place.

Giza

People To Meet

Explain why this person is important.

King Khufu

Academic Vocabulary

Define these academic vocabulary words from this lesson.

structure

principle

Sum It Up

What was the purpose of pyramids?

Section Wrap-up

Now that you have read the section, write the answers to the questions that were included in* Setting a Purpose for Reading *at the beginning of the lesson.

What were the main Egyptian beliefs about deities and the afterlife?

Why did Egyptians build pyramids?

Chapter 2, Section 3
The Egyptian Empire

(Pages 59–67)

Main Idea

Setting a Purpose for Reading Think about these questions as you read:

- What was life like during the Middle Kingdom?
- What important events happened during the New Kingdom?

Reading Strategy

As you read pages 65–67 in your textbook, complete this diagram showing the major accomplishments of Ramses II.

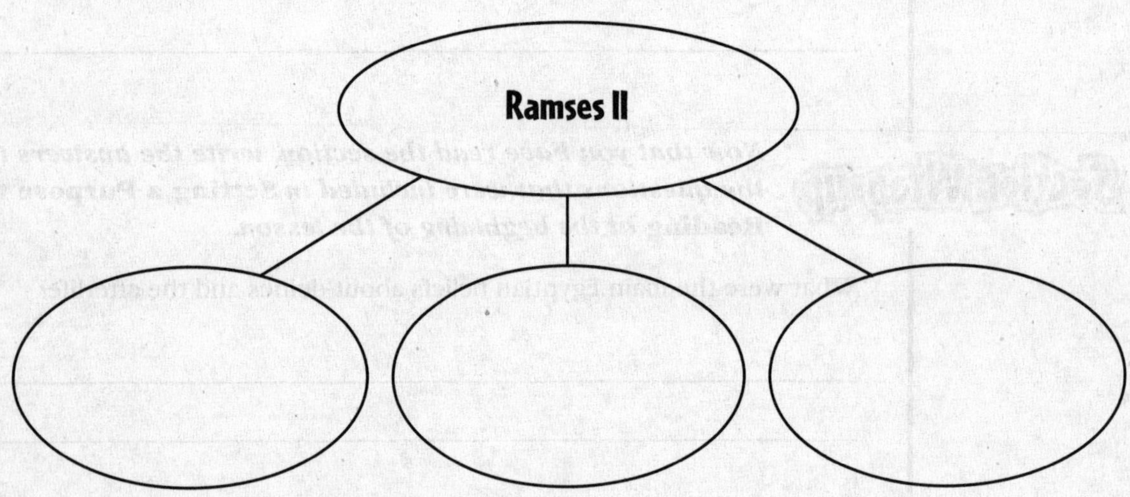

The Middle Kingdom *(pages 60–61)*

Skimming

The Middle Kingdom was a golden age for Egypt. Before you read, skim the passage. Make a note of any points that support this statement. Then, after you read, go back and fill in additional information about this golden age.

Terms To Know

Define or describe the following term from this lesson.

tribute

Places To Locate

Briefly describe the following place.

Thebes

People To Meet

Explain why this person is important.

Ahmose

Academic Vocabulary

Define these academic vocabulary words from this lesson.

restore

create

Sum It Up

Who were the Hyksos?

The New Kingdom *(pages 61–62)*

Evaluating

As you read, list the achievements of Hatshepsut and Thutmose III in the columns below. Then, based on the achievements you have listed, write a short paragraph evaluating the leadership of one of these rulers. Use specific examples from your list to support your opinion.

Hatshepsut	Thutmose III

Evaluation

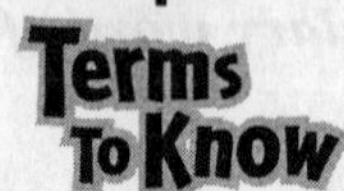

Define or describe the following term from this lesson.

incense

Academic Vocabulary

Define these academic vocabulary words from this lesson.

priority

behalf

Terms To Review

Use this term, that you studied earlier, in a sentence that reflects the term's meaning.

pharaoh
(Chapter 2, Section 2)

Sum It Up

Describe Egyptian trade during the rule of Hatshepsut.

The Legacies of Two Pharaohs *(pages 64–65)*

Questioning

Before you read, skim the text. Then write three questions about the main ideas you find. After you have finished reading, write the answers to these questions.

1.

Key Points | Notes

2.

3.

People To Meet

Explain why this person is important.

Akhenaton

Academic Vocabulary

Define these academic vocabulary words from this lesson.

maintain

rely

Sum It Up

Why is Tutankhamen so famous today?

The End of the New Kingdom *(pages 65–67)*

Sequencing

As you read, place the following events in the correct order by numbering them in the spaces provided.

1. ____ Groups from the eastern Mediterranean attack Egypt by sea.

2. ____ Egyptian armies regain lands in western Asia.

3. ____ Egypt is taken over by the Assyrians.

4. ____ Egypt is conquered by Libyans.

5. ____ Ramses II becomes pharaoh.

6. ____ Egypt is ruled by Kush.

7. ____ The temple at Karnak is built.

People To Meet

Explain why this person is important.

Ramses II

____

____

Academic Vocabulary

Define this academic vocabulary word from this lesson.

construct

____

____

Sum It Up

What groups conquered Egypt starting in the 900s B.C.?

____

____

____

Now that you have read the section, write the answers to the questions that were included in* Setting a Purpose for Reading *at the beginning of the lesson.

What was life like during the Middle Kingdom?

What important events happened during the New Kingdom?

Chapter 2, Section 4
The Civilization of Kush

(Pages 68–72)

Main Idea

Setting a Purpose for Reading Think about these questions as you read:

- Who were the Nubians and what were they known for?
- What was life like for the people of Kush?

Reading Strategy

As you read pages 70–72 in your textbook, complete this diagram to show the differences and similarities between Napata and Meroë.

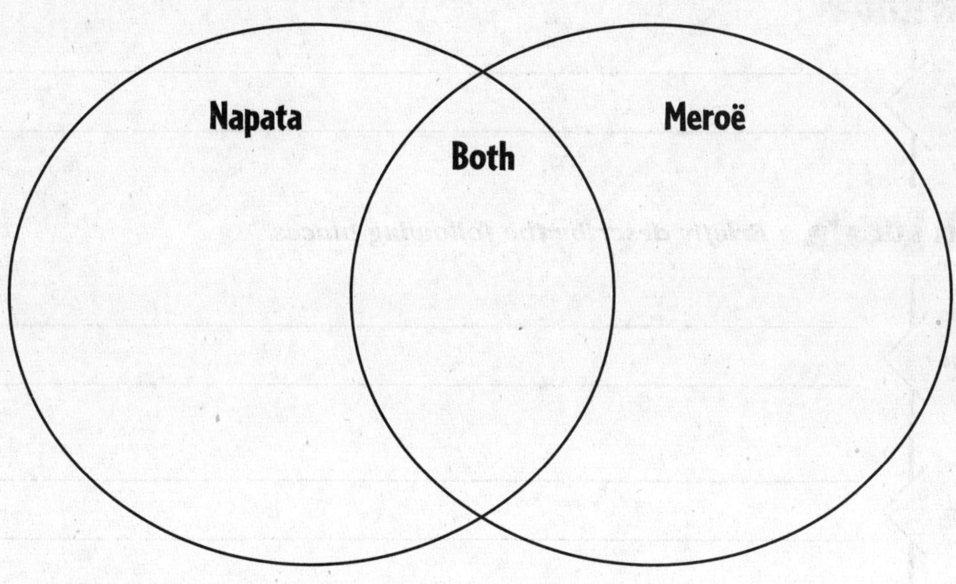

Key Points

Nubia *(pages 69–70)*

Determining the Main Idea

As you read, write the main idea of the passage. Review your statement when you have finished reading and revise as needed.

Terms To Know

Define or describe the following term from this lesson.

savanna

Places To Locate

Briefly describe the following places.

Nubia

Kush

Kerma

Academic Vocabulary

Define these academic vocabulary words from this lesson.

period

collapse

Terms To Review

Use each of these terms, that you studied earlier, in a sentence that reflects the term's meaning.

historian
(Chapter 2, Section 2)

hieroglyphics
(Chapter 2, Section 2)

Sum It Up

Where was Kush located?

The Rise of Kush *(pages 70–72)*

Outlining ***Complete this outline as you read.***

I. The Importance of Iron

A. ____________________

B. ____________________

II. A New Capital

A. ____________________

B. ____________________

III. Building a Profitable Trade

A. ____________________

B. ____________________

Places To Locate ***Briefly describe the following places.***

Napata ____________________

Meroë ____________________

People To Meet ***Explain why each of these people is important.***

Kashta ____________________

Piye ____________________

Academic Vocabulary

Define these academic vocabulary words from this lesson

decline

culture

Terms To Review

Use each of these terms that you studied earlier in a sentence that reflects the term's meaning.

caravan
(Chapter 1, Section 3)

dynasty
(Chapter 2, Section 1)

Sum It Up

How did Kush become a wealthy kingdom?

Now that you have read the section, write the answers to the questions that were included in* Setting a Purpose for Reading *at the beginning of the lesson.

Who were the Nubians and what were they known for?

What was life like for the people of Kush?

Chapter 3, Section 1
The First Israelites

(Pages 80–85)

Main Idea

Setting a Purpose for Reading Think about these questions as you read:

- What did the Israelites believe?
- Where was the Promised Land of the Israelites, and how did they return there?

Reading Strategy

As you read pages 81–85 in your textbook, complete this sequence chart to trace the movement of the Israelites.

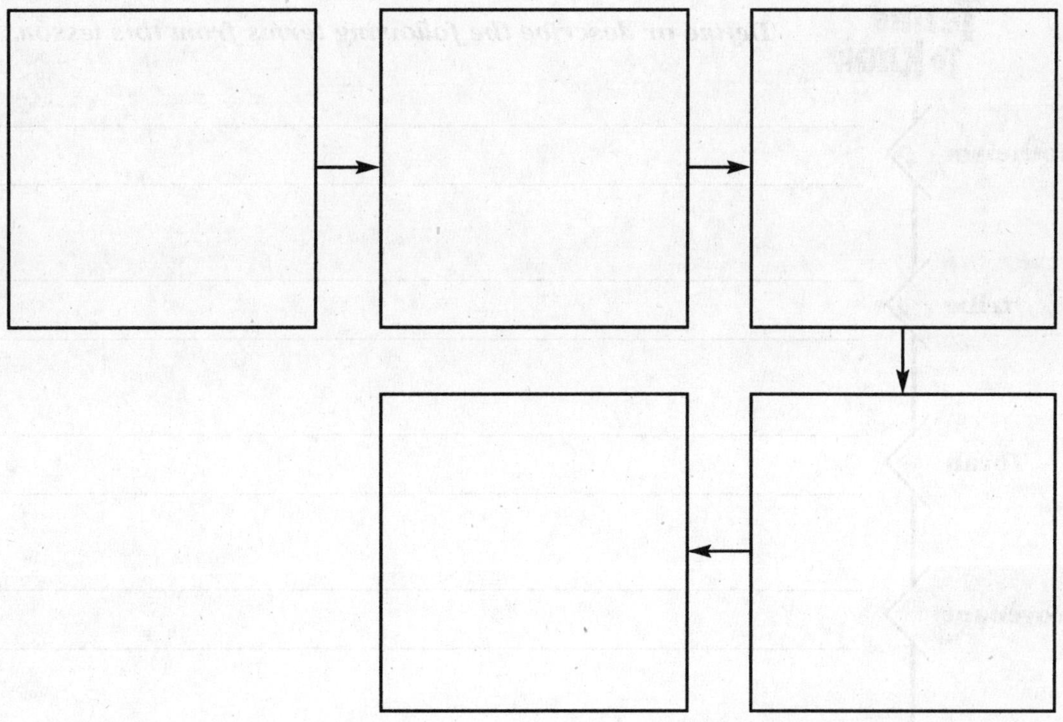

The Early Israelites *(pages 81–83)*

Connecting

As you read, consider how Judaism has influenced values in your culture today. Summarize your thoughts in a paragraph. Be sure to include specific ways that you see the values and beliefs of Judaism reflected in your world.

Terms To Know

Define or describe the following terms from this lesson.

monotheism

tribe

Torah

covenant

People To Meet

Explain why these people are important.

Abraham

Jacob

Moses

Academic Vocabulary

Define these academic vocabulary words from this lesson.

focus

occupy

Terms To Review

Use this term that you studied earlier in a sentence that reflects the term's meaning.

pharaoh
(Chapter 2, Section 2)

Sum It Up

What covenant was described in the Torah?

The Promised Land *(pages 84–85)*

Responding

As you read the story of Joshua and Jericho, record your responses. What do you think about the story? What questions do you have? What do you learn about the Israelites and about Joshua? After reading the section, write a short paragraph summarizing your response to the story.

Terms To Know

Define or describe the following term from this lesson.

alphabet

People To Meet

Explain why these people are important.

Phoenicians

Deborah

Academic Vocabulary

Define this academic vocabulary word from this lesson.

create

Use this term that you studied earlier in a sentence that reflects the term's meaning.

tribe
(Chapter 3, Section 1)

Sum It Up

Who led the Israelites into Canaan, and what city did they conquer under his leadership?

Section Wrap-up

Now that you have read the section, write the answers to the questions that were included in* Setting a Purpose for Reading *at the beginning of the lesson.

What did the Israelites believe?

Where was the Promised Land of the Israelites, and how did they return there?

Chapter 3, Section 2
The Kingdom of Israel

(Pages 86–92)

Main Idea

Setting a Purpose for Reading Think about these questions as you read:

- Why did the Israelites choose to follow kings instead of judges?
- Who was King David and why was he important?
- Why were the Israelites conquered?

Reading Strategy

As you read pages 87–92 in your textbook, complete this chart to list the characteristics of Israel and Judah.

Location		
Capital City		
Date Conquered		
Conquered By		

The Israelites Choose a King *(page 87)*

Determining the Main Idea

As you read, write the main idea of the passage. Review your statement when you have finished reading and revise as needed.

Terms To Know

Define or describe the following term from this lesson.

prophet

People To Meet

Explain why these people are important.

Philistines

Saul

David

Academic Vocabulary

Define this academic vocabulary word from this lesson.

instruct

Sum It Up *Why did the Israelites want a king?*

____

____

____

____

David and Solomon *(pages 89–90)*

Summarizing ***As you read, complete the following sentences. Doing so will help you summarize the section.***

1. David defeated the giant Philistine named ______________ with a ______________. As David won more victories ______________ became jealous and plotted to ______________ David.

2. David took over the throne in about ______________, when Saul and his sons were ______________ in battle.

3. David created an empire and established the capital of ______________. His son ______________ built a great temple there.

4. When Solomon died, the 12 tribes broke into two nations: ______________ and ______________.

Terms To Know ***Define or describe the following terms from this lesson.***

empire ____

____

tribute

proverbs

Places To Locate *Briefly describe the following places.*

Jerusalem

Judah

Academic Vocabulary *Define these academic vocabulary words from this lesson.*

expand

symbol

Sum It Up *Why did Solomon tax the people so heavily?*

Key Points

Notes

A Troubled Time *(pages 90–92)*

Sequencing ***As you read, place the following events in the correct order by numbering them in the spaces provided.***

1. ____ The Egyptians conquer Judah
2. ____ The Jews unite with the Egyptians to fight the Chaldeans
3. ____ King Nebuchadnezzar captures Jerusalem
4. ____ The Assyrians conquer Israel and scatter the 10 tribes
5. ____ Nebuchadnezzar takes the Jews into captivity in Babylon
6. ____ The Assyrians become known as Samaritans and eventually worship Israel's God
7. ____ The Chaldeans conquer Egypt

People To Meet ***Explain why this person is important.***

Nebuchadnezzar ____

____

Academic Vocabulary ***Define this academic vocabulary word from this lesson.***

route ____

____

Sum It Up ***Why did the Assyrians and Chaldeans want to control the land belonging to the Israelites?***

____

____

____

____

Now that you have read the section, write the answers to the questions that were included in* Setting a Purpose for Reading *at the beginning of the lesson.

Why did the Israelites choose to follow kings instead of judges?

Who was King David and why was he important?

Why were the Israelites conquered?

Chapter 3, Section 3
The Growth of Judaism

(Pages 93–102)

Main Idea

Setting a Purpose for Reading Think about these questions as you read:

- How did Judaism grow in the period following their exile?
- Why did the Romans destroy the temple and exile the Jews?

Reading Strategy

As you read page 96 in your textbook, complete this diagram to describe the Maccabees.

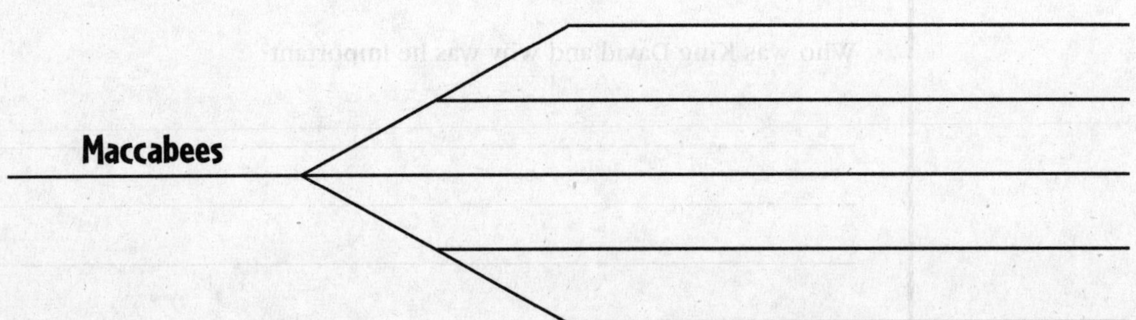

Exile and Return *(pages 94–95)*

Outlining

Complete this outline as you read.

I. Why Did Jews Return to Judah?

A. ______________________________

B. ______________________________

II. What Is in the Hebrew Bible?

A. ______________________________

B. ______________________________

III. The Jews Look to the Future

A. ______________________________

B. ______________________________

Terms To Know

Define or describe the following terms from this lesson.

exile ______________________________

Sabbath ______________________________

synagogue ______________________________

Places To Locate

Briefly describe the following place.

Babylon ______________________________

Key Points | Notes

Academic Vocabulary

Define these academic vocabulary words from this lesson.

series

symbol

Terms To Review

Use this term that you studied earlier in a sentence that reflects the term's meaning.

scribe
(Chapter 1, Section 2)

Sum It Up

Who allowed the Jews to return to Judah?

The Jews and the Greeks *(pages 95–96)*

Questioning

As you read, write three questions about the main ideas presented in the text. After you have finished reading, write the answers to these questions.

1.

2. ______

3. ______

Terms To Know

Define or describe the following term from this lesson.

Diaspora

People To Meet

Explain why this person is important.

Judas Maccabeus

Academic Vocabulary

Define these academic vocabulary words from this lesson.

version

trace

Notes

Sum It Up

How did Alexander the Great affect the Israelites?

The Jewish Way of Life *(pages 97–98)*

Determining the Main Idea

As you read, complete the chart below to identify the main ideas from your reading.

The Jewish Way of Life

Academic Vocabulary

Define these academic vocabulary words from this lesson.

affect

community

Sum It Up

Why were sons especially valued in Jewish society?

The Jews and the Romans *(pages 100–102)*

Monitoring Comprehension

As you read, answer these questions to be sure you understand the main ideas of the section.

1. What did Herod do as king?

2. Why were the Jews unable to regain control over their Roman rulers?

3. Who were the Pharisees?

4. Who were the Sadducees?

5. Who were the Essenes?

6. What were the cause and results of the Jewish revolts?

7. What role did rabbis play in Jewish society?

Terms To Know

Define or describe the following terms from this lesson.

messiah

rabbi

People To Meet

Explain why each of these people is important.

Herod

Zealots

Yohanan ben Zaccai

Academic Vocabulary

Define these academic vocabulary words from this lesson.

expand

despite

Sum It Up

How did the Roman conquest affect the Jews?

Now that you have read the section, write the answers to the questions that were included in* Setting a Purpose for Reading *at the beginning of the lesson.

How did Judaism grow in the period following their exile?

____

____

____

____

____

____

Why did the Romans destroy the temple and exile the Jews?

____

____

____

____

____

____

Chapter 4, Section 1

The Early Greeks

(Pages 116–123)

Main Idea

Setting a Purpose for Reading Think about these questions as you read:

- How did early Greek kingdoms develop?
- What ideas developed in Greek city-states?

Reading Strategy

As you read pages 122–123 in your textbook, complete this diagram by filling in details about the polis.

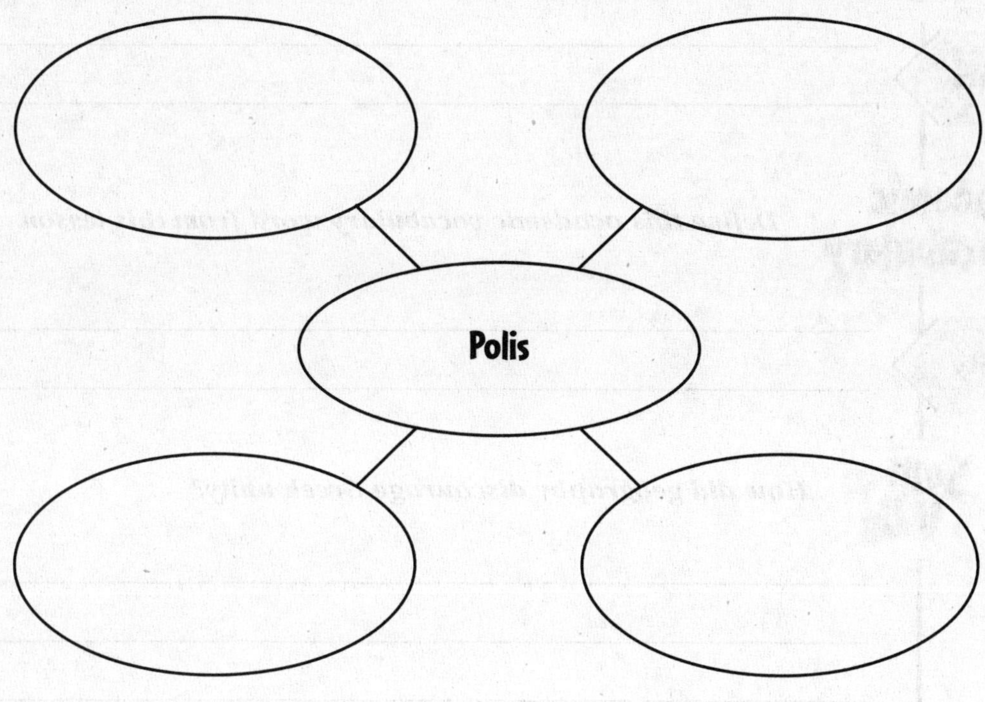

The Geography of Greece *(page 117)*

Visualizing

As you read, list words and phrases that help you picture the land of Greece. Now imagine you are a Greek sailor or trader. Write a paragraph in your own words about what you see around you.

Terms To Know

Define or describe the following key term from this lesson.

peninsula

Academic Vocabulary

Define this academic vocabulary word from this lesson.

community

Sum It Up

How did geography discourage Greek unity?

The Minoans *(page 118)*

Questioning

Before you read, skim the section and write three questions about the main ideas you find. After you have finished reading, write the answers to these questions.

1. ______________________________

____

____

____

2. ______________________________

____

____

____

3. ______________________________

____

____

____

Academic Vocabulary

Define this academic vocabulary word from this lesson.

region ______________________________

____

Terms To Review

Use each of these terms that you studied earlier in a sentence that reflects the term's meaning.

archaeologist
(Chapter 1, Section 1)

civilization
(Chapter 1, Section 2)

Sum It Up

How did the Minoans become a trading civilization?

The First Greek Kingdoms *(pages 119–120)*

Outlining

Complete this outline as you read.

I. What Were Mycenaean Kingdoms Like?

A.

B.

II. Power From Trade and War

A.

B.

III. What Was the Dark Age?

A.

B.

People To Meet

Explain why this person is important.

Agamemnon

Places To Locate

Briefly describe the following places.

Mycenae

Peloponnesus

Academic Vocabulary

Define these academic vocabulary words from this lesson.

positive

culture

Terms To Review

Use each of these terms that you studied earlier in a sentence that reflects the term's meaning.

historian
(Chapter 1, Section 1)

artisan
(Chapter 1, Section 2)

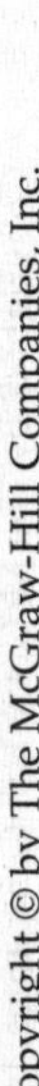

Notes

Sum It Up

What changes occurred during the Dark Age in ancient Greece?

A Move to Colonize *(page 121)*

Determining the Main Idea

As you read, write the main idea of the passage. Review your statement when you have finished reading and revise as needed.

Terms To Know

Define or describe the following term from this lesson.

colony

Academic Vocabulary

Define these academic vocabulary words from this lesson.

culture

overseas

Sum It Up *How did new Greek colonies affect industry?*

The Polis *(pages 122–123)*

Previewing *To preview this section, first skim the section, looking for headings and main ideas. Then write a sentence or two explaining what you think you will be learning. After you have finished reading, revise your statements as necessary.*

Terms To Know *Define or describe the following terms from this lesson.*

polis

agora

Academic Vocabulary *Define these academic vocabulary words from this lesson.*

vary

debate

Use this term that you studied earlier in a sentence that reflects the term's meaning.

city-state
(Chapter 1, Section 2)

Sum It Up

How did citizenship make the Greeks different from other ancient peoples?

Section Wrap-up

Now that you have read the section, write the answers to the questions that were included in* Setting a Purpose for Reading *at the beginning of the lesson.

How did early Greek kingdoms develop?

What ideas developed in Greek city-states?

Chapter 4, Section 2
Sparta and Athens
(Pages 124–130)

Main Idea

Setting a Purpose for Reading Think about these questions as you read:

- Why did Spartans conquer and control groups of people?
- How were the people of Athens different from the people of Sparta?

Reading Strategy

As you read pages 125–130 in your textbook, complete this graphic organizer comparing and contrasting life in Sparta and Athens.

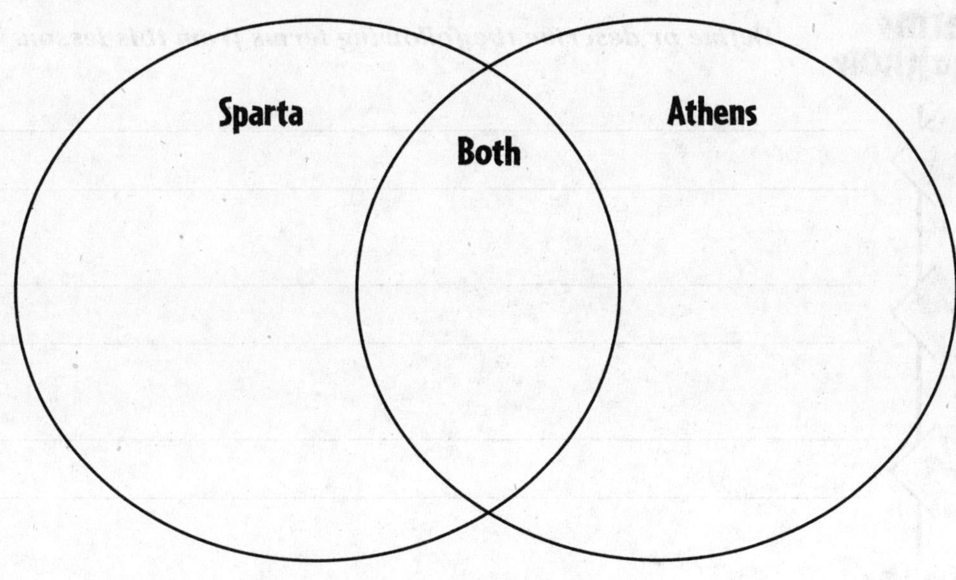

Tyranny in the City-States *(pages 125–126)*

Summarizing

As you read, complete the following sentences. Doing so will help you summarize the section.

1. _______________, _______________, and _______________ all wanted a part in Greek government. Their unhappiness led to the rise of _______________, men who took power by force. These tyrants took power away from the _______________.

2. Most Greeks wanted all _______________ to be a part of the government. So most city-states became either _______________ or _______________.

Terms To Know

Define or describe the following terms from this lesson.

tyrant ____

oligarchy ____

democracy ____

Academic Vocabulary

Define these academic vocabulary words from this lesson.

structure ____

participate ____

Sum It Up *Why were tyrants popular in the city-states?*

Sparta (pages 126–127)

Drawing Conclusions ***As you read, write three details about the Spartans. Then write a general statement or conclusion about the Spartans based on these details.***

1. ______________________________

2. ______________________________

3. ______________________________

General Statement

Key Points | **Notes**

Terms To Know

Define or describe the following term from this lesson.

helots

Academic Vocabulary

Define this academic vocabulary word from this lesson.

enforce

Terms To Review

Use this term that you studied earlier in a sentence that reflects the term's meaning.

oligarchy
(Chapter 4, Section 2)

Sum It Up

Why did the Spartans stress military training?

Athens *(pages 128–130)*

Connecting

What do you know about your state and national government? Think about things you have seen or read in the news. As you read, compare your state and national government with the democracy of Athens. Summarize your thoughts in a paragraph. Be sure to address the similarities and differences that you see.

Academic Vocabulary

Define these academic vocabulary words from this lesson.

nonetheless

process

Terms To Review

Use this term that you studied earlier in a sentence that reflects the term's meaning.

democracy
(Chapter 4, Section 2)

Sum It Up

How did Cleisthenes build a democracy in Athens?

Section Wrap-up

Now that you have read the section, write the answers to the questions that were included in* Setting a Purpose for Reading *at the beginning of the lesson.

Why did Spartans conquer and control groups of people?

How were the people of Athens different from the people of Sparta?

Chapter 4, Section 3
Persia Attacks the Greeks

(Pages 131–137)

Main Idea

Setting a Purpose for Reading Think about these questions as you read:

- How did the Persian Empire bring together such a wide area?
- What role did Athens and Sparta play in defeating the Persians?

Reading Strategy

As you read pages 132–137 in your textbook, complete this graphic organizer listing the accomplishments of Cyrus, Darius, and Xerxes.

Ruler	Accomplishments
Cyrus	
Darius	
Xerxes	

The Persian Empire *(pages 132–133)*

Outlining ***Complete this outline as you read.***

I. The Rise of the Persian Empire

A. ______

B. ______

II. What Was Persian Government Like?

A. ______

B. ______

III. The Persian Religion

A. ______

B. ______

Terms To Know ***Define or describe the following terms from this lesson.***

satrapies ______

satrap ______

Zoroastrianism ______

People To Meet ***Explain why this person is important.***

Cyrus the Great ______

Academic Vocabulary

Define these academic vocabulary words from this lesson.

vision

dominate

Terms To Review

Use each of these terms that you studied earlier in a sentence that reflects the term's meaning.

nomad
(Chapter 1, Section 1)

empire
(Chapter 1, Section 2)

Sum It Up

Why did Darius create satrapies?

The Persian Wars *(pages 134–137)*

Sequencing

As you read, number the following events in the correct order.

1. ____ Greek army crushed the Persian army at Plataea

2. ____ Persian fleet landed 20,000 soldiers on the plain of Marathon

3. ____ Athenian army helped the Greeks in Asia Minor rebel against Persian rulers

4. ____ Xerxes launches invasion of Greece

5. ____ Alexander invades the Persian Empire

6. ____ Darius dies

Places To Locate

Briefly describe the following places.

Marathon

Thermopylae

Salamis

Plataea

People To Meet

Explain why each of these people is important.

Xerxes

Themistocles

Academic Vocabulary

Define this academic vocabulary word from this lesson.

internal

Sum It Up

What led to the Persian Wars?

Section Wrap-up

Now that you have read the section, write the answers to the questions that were included in* Setting a Purpose for Reading *at the beginning of the lesson.

How did the Persian Empire bring together such a wide area?

What role did Athens and Sparta play in defeating the Persians?

Chapter 4, Section 4
The Age of Pericles

(Pages 138–146)

Main Idea

Setting a Purpose for Reading Think about these questions as you read:

- How did Athens change under the rule of Pericles?
- What happened when Sparta and Athens went to war for control of Greece?

Reading Strategy

As you read pages 139–144 in your textbook, create a circle graph showing how many citizens, foreigners, and enslaved people lived in Athens in the 400s B.C.

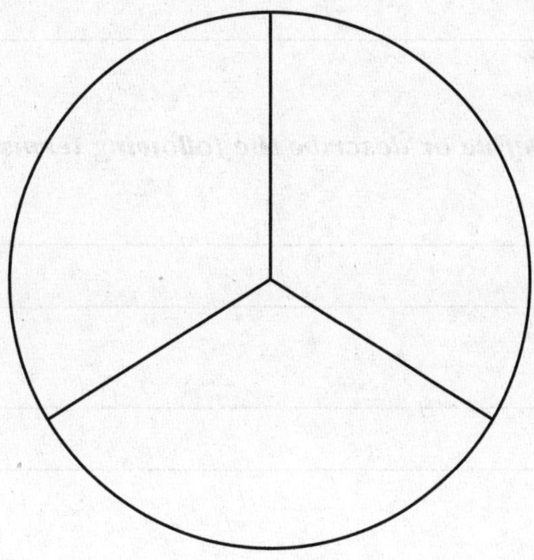

The Athenian Empire *(pages 139–140)*

Evaluating

What do you think makes a leader great? Think of leaders you have known or heard about. Then, as you read, list the achievements of Pericles. Based on the achievements you have listed, write a paragraph evaluating his leadership. Use specific examples from your list to support your opinion.

Terms To Know

Define or describe the following terms from this lesson.

direct democracy

representative democracy

philosophers

Places To Locate

Briefly describe the following place.

Delos

People To Meet *Explain why this person is important.*

Pericles

Academic Vocabulary *Define these academic vocabulary words from this lesson.*

behalf

achieve

Sum It Up *What is the difference between a direct democracy and a representative democracy?*

Daily Life in Athens *(pages 142–144)*

Questioning *What was life like in Athens? Before you read, skim the reading to identify main ideas. Then write three questions you think your reading will answer. After you have finished reading, write the answers to these questions.*

1.

Key Points | Notes

2.

3.

People To Meet

Explain why this person is important.

Aspasia

Academic Vocabulary

Define these academic vocabulary words from this lesson.

economy

philosophy

Sum It Up

How did Athenian men and women spend their time?

The Peloponnesian War *(pages 144–146)*

Predicting

Before you read, based on what you know about Sparta and Athens, predict who you think will win the war. Support your prediction with facts from your reading. After you read, write a paragraph about your reaction to the actual outcome.

Academic Vocabulary

Define these academic vocabulary words from this lesson.

framework

cooperate

Terms To Review

Use this term that you studied earlier in a sentence that reflects the term's meaning.

colony
(Chapter 4, Section 1)

Sum It Up

What effects did the Peloponnesian War have on Greece?

Section Wrap-up

Now that you have read the section, write the answers to the questions that were included in* Setting a Purpose for Reading *at the beginning of the lesson.

How did Athens change under the rule of Pericles?

What happened when Sparta and Athens went to war for control of Greece?

Chapter 5, Section 1
The Culture of Ancient Greece

(Pages 154–163)

Main Idea

Setting a Purpose for Reading Think about these questions as you read:

- What were the main religious beliefs of the Greeks?
- How did Greek art and architecture reflect Greek ideas?

Reading Strategy

As you read pages 155–159 in your textbook, complete this Venn diagram showing the similarities and differences between an epic and a fable.

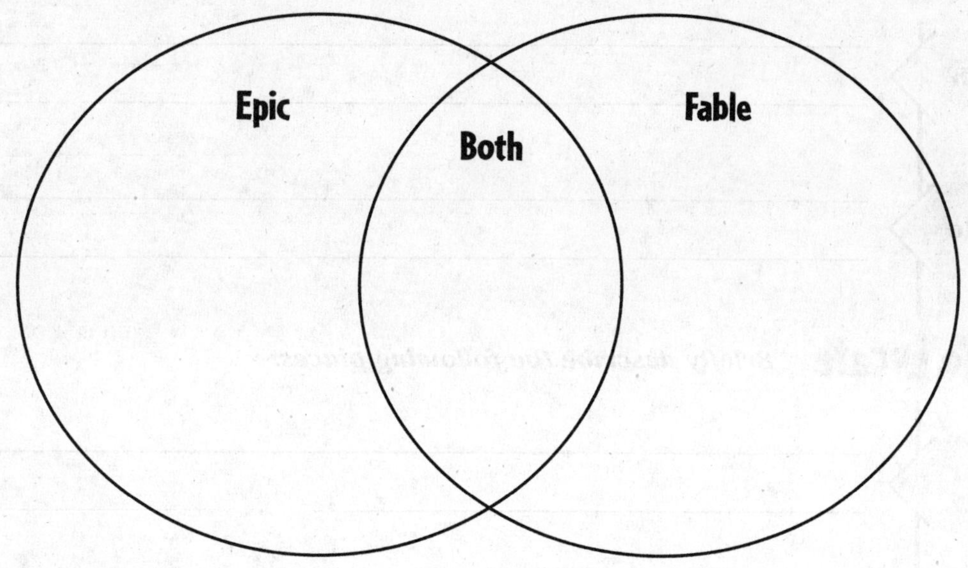

Greek Mythology *(pages 155–156)*

Previewing

Have you ever read a Greek myth? Preview this section to get an idea of what is ahead. First, skim the section. Then write a sentence or two explaining what you think you will be learning. After you have finished reading, revise your statements as necessary.

Terms To Know

Define or describe the following terms from this lesson.

myth

oracle

Places To Locate

Briefly describe the following places.

Mount Olympus

Delphi

Notes

Academic Vocabulary

Define these academic vocabulary words from this lesson.

affect

grant

Terms To Review

Use this term that you studied earlier in a sentence that reflects the term's meaning.

empire
(Chapter 3, Section 2)

Sum It Up

Why did the Greeks have rituals and festivals for their gods and goddesses?

Greek Poetry and Fables *(pages 157–158)*

Summarizing

As you read, write one sentence summarizing each of the following stories and fables.

The *Odyssey*

The *Iliad*

"The Tortoise and the Hare"

Terms To Know

Define or describe the following terms from this lesson.

epic

fable

People To Meet

Explain why each of these people is important.

Homer

Aesop

Academic Vocabulary

Define these academic vocabulary words from this lesson.

generation

tradition

Sum It Up

What are the characteristics of a fable?

Greek Drama *(pages 160–161)*

Connecting

What are your favorite television shows and movies? As you read, compare the dramas, comedies, and tragedies you watch with Greek drama. Summarize your thoughts in a paragraph. Be sure to address the similarities and differences that you see.

Terms To Know

Define or describe the following terms from this lesson.

drama

tragedy

comedy

People To Meet

Explain why each of these people is important.

Sophocles

Euripides

Academic Vocabulary

Define the following academic vocabulary word from this lesson.

conflict

Sum It Up

What two types of drama did the Greeks create?

Greek Art and Architecture *(pages 162–163)*

Synthesizing

As you read, find information to answer the first two questions. Then use these answers to respond to the third question below.

1. What beliefs and ideas are reflected in Greek art and architecture?

2. Where do we see examples of Greek architecture today?

3. Synthesize: How has ancient Greece influenced our culture today?

Academic Vocabulary

Define these academic vocabulary words from this lesson.

structure

version

Sum It Up

What was the most important type of building in ancient Greece?

Section Wrap-up

Now that you have read the section, write the answers to the questions that were included in* Setting a Purpose for Reading *at the beginning of the lesson.

What were the main religious beliefs of the Greeks?

How did Greek art and architecture reflect Greek ideas?

Chapter 5, Section 2
Greek Philosophy and History

(Pages 168–173)

Main Idea

Setting a Purpose for Reading Think about these questions as you read:

- What ideas did Greek philosophers develop?
- How did Greeks contribute to the history of Western civilization?

Reading Strategy

As you read pages 169–171 in your textbook, complete diagrams like this one to show the basic philosophies of Socrates.

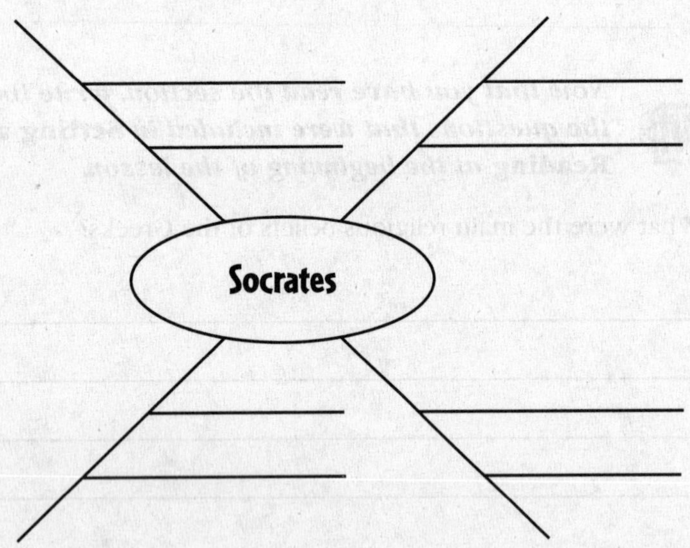

Greek Philosophers *(pages 169–171)*

Reviewing

Complete the following reading guide by filling in the important ideas from each of these Greek philosophers. Use your guide to review main points from your reading.

Philosopher	Ideas
Pythagoras	
Socrates	
Plato	
Aristotle	

Terms To Know

Define or describe the following terms from this lesson.

philosophy

philosopher

Sophist

Socratic method

Academic Vocabulary

Define these academic vocabulary words from this lesson.

reject

method

Terms To Review

Use each of these terms that you studied earlier in a sentence that reflects the term's meaning.

tyrant
(Chapter 4, Section 2)

oligarchy
(Chapter 4, Section 2)

Sum It Up

How did Aristotle's idea of government differ from Plato's?

Greek Historians *(page 173)*

Skimming

Quickly look over the entire selection to get a general idea about the reading. Then briefly describe what the selection is about on the lines below.

People To Meet

Explain why each of these people is important.

Herodotus

Thucydides

Academic Vocabulary

Define these academic vocabulary words from this lesson.

accurate

stress

Sum It Up

How did Thucydides view war and politics?

Section Wrap-up

Now that you have read the section, write the answers to the questions that were included in* Setting a Purpose for Reading *at the beginning of the lesson.

What ideas did Greek philosophers develop?

How did Greeks contribute to the history of Western civilization?

Chapter 5, Section 3
Alexander the Great

(Pages 174–179)

Main Idea

Setting a Purpose for Reading Think about these questions as you read:

- How did Philip II of Macedonia unite the Greek states?
- How did Alexander the Great change history?

Reading Strategy

As you read pages 176–179 in your textbook, complete this diagram to track the achievements of Alexander the Great.

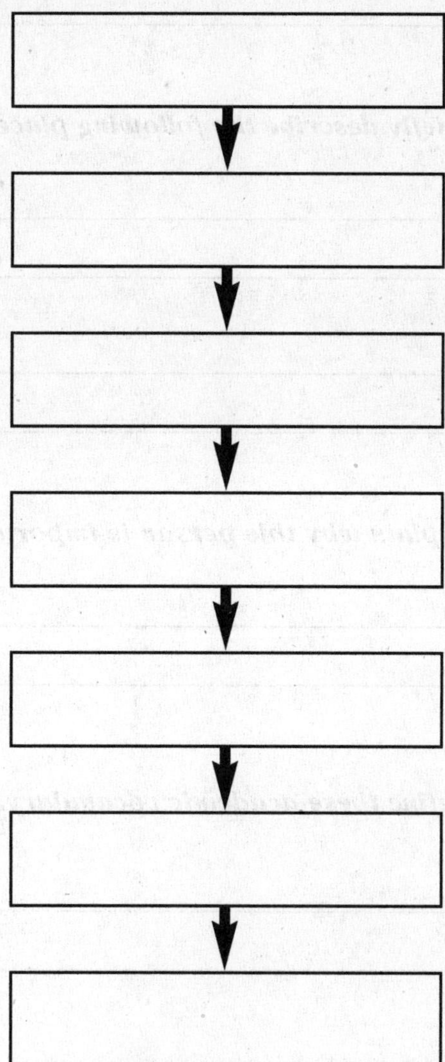

Macedonia Attacks Greece *(pages 175–176)*

Predicting

Think about all you have learned about Greece up to this point. Now, before you read, answer the question below. What do you predict will happen? After you read, write a brief paragraph about your reaction to the actual events.

Will Macedonia defeat the Greeks?

Places To Locate

Briefly describe the following places.

Macedonia

Chaeronea

People To Meet

Explain why this person is important.

Philip II

Academic Vocabulary

Define these academic vocabulary words from this lesson.

achieve

decline

Sum It Up *Why did Philip II invade Greece?*

Alexander Builds an Empire *(pages 176–179)*

Previewing ***Look at the headings and write a question about each one. Find answers to your questions as you read. Revise your question if the answer is not found in the reading.***

I. Alexander Builds an Empire

II. Alexander's Conquests

III. Alexander's Legacy

IV. The Empire Breaks Apart

Terms To Know ***Define or describe the following terms from this lesson.***

legacy

Hellenistic Era

Places To Locate

Briefly describe the following places.

Syria

Alexandria

Academic Vocabulary

Define these academic vocabulary words from this lesson.

create

military

Terms To Review

Use this term that you studied earlier in a sentence that reflects the term's meaning.

satrap
(Chapter 4, Section 3)

Sum It Up

What was Alexander's legacy?

Now that you have read the section, write the answers to the questions that were included in* Setting a Purpose for Reading *at the beginning of the lesson.

How did Philip II of Macedonia unite the Greek states?

How did Alexander the Great change history?

Chapter 5, Section 4
The Spread of Greek Culture

(Pages 182–186)

Main Idea

Setting a Purpose for Reading Think about these questions as you read:

- How did Greek culture spread and develop in the Hellenistic Era?
- Who were Epicurus and Zeno?

Reading Strategy

As you read pages 183–186 in your textbook, create a diagram to show the major Greek contributions to Western civilization.

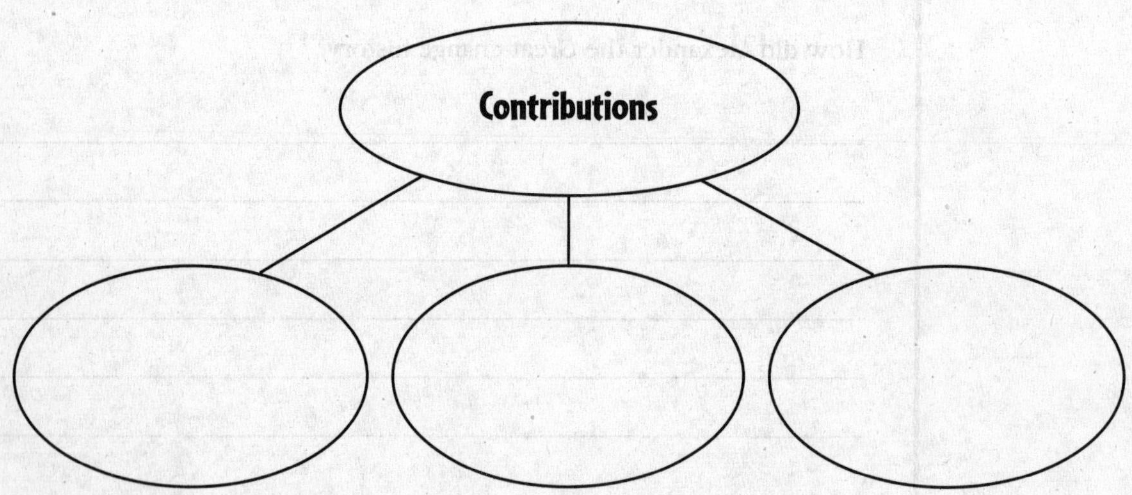

Greek Culture Spreads *(page 183)*

Determining the Main Idea

As you read, list the causes and effects of the spread of Greek culture in the Hellenistic Era.

Greek Culture Spreads	
Causes	**Effects**

Sum It Up

How did the Hellenistic kingdoms spread Greek culture?

Philosophy *(page 184)*

Responding

What is true happiness and what really makes people happy in life? Consider the views of the Epicureans and the Stoics. Then write a paragraph responding to their views and stating your own views about personal happiness.

Terms To Know

Define or describe the following terms from this lesson.

Epicureanism

Stoicism

Academic Vocabulary

Define these two academic vocabulary words.

goal

lecture

Terms To Review

Use each of these terms that you studied earlier in a sentence that reflects the term's meaning.

philosopher
(Chapter 5, Section 2)

philosophy
(Chapter 5, Section 2)

Sum It Up

What were the differences between Epicureanism and Stoicism?

Greek Science and Math *(pages 185–186)*

Monitoring Comprehension

As you read, list the major contributions made by Hellenistic mathematicians and astronomers in the graphic organizer below.

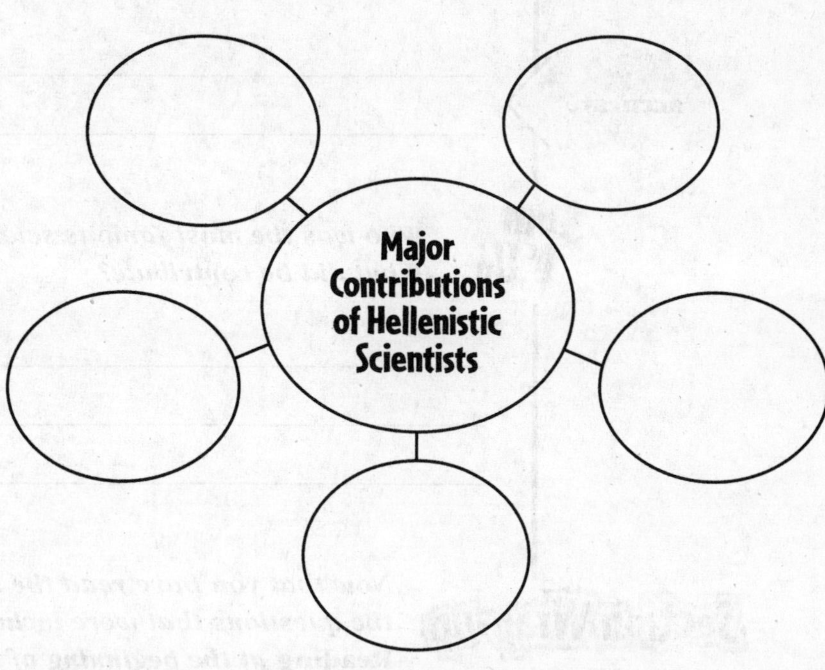

Terms To Know

Define or describe the following terms from this lesson.

astronomer

plane geometry

solid geometry

Academic Vocabulary

Define these academic vocabulary words from this lesson.

major

accurate

Sum It Up

Who was the most famous scientist of the Hellenistic Era? What did he contribute?

Section Wrap-up

Now that you have read the section, write the answers to the questions that were included in* Setting a Purpose for Reading *at the beginning of the lesson.

How did Greek culture spread and develop in the Hellenistic Era?

Who were Epicurus and Zeno?

Chapter 6, Section 1

India's Early Civilization

(Pages 194–201)

Main Idea

Setting a Purpose for Reading Think about these questions as you read:

- What factors influenced the rise of India's early civilization?
- How did the Aryans change life in India?

Reading Strategy

As you read pages 195–201 in your textbook, complete this diagram to show how the Aryans changed India.

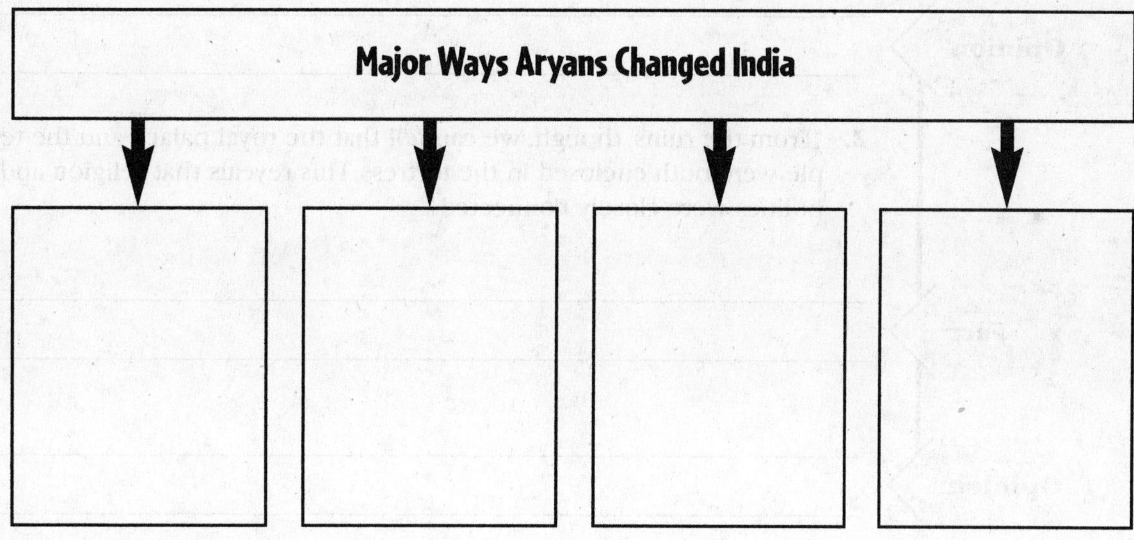

The Land of India *(pages 195–197)*

Evaluating

Look at the following statements from your reading. Evaluate each to determine which parts are facts and which parts are opinions.

1. "These ancient city dwellers had some surprising conveniences. Wells supplied water, and residents even had indoor bathrooms. Wastewater flowed to drains under the streets, running through pipes to pits outside the city walls. Houses also had garbage chutes connected to a bin in the street. It is likely the city government was well organized to be able to provide so many services."

Fact

Opinion

2. "From the ruins, though, we can tell that the royal palace and the temple were both enclosed in the fortress. This reveals that religion and politics were closely connected."

Fact

Opinion

Terms To Know

Define or describe the following terms from this lesson.

subcontinent

monsoon

Academic Vocabulary

Define this academic vocabulary word from this lesson.

similar

Terms To Review

Use this term that you studied earlier in a sentence that reflects the term's meaning.

archaeologist
(Chapter 1, Section 1)

Sum It Up

How is India separated from the rest of Asia?

The Aryans *(pages 198–199)*

Summarizing

As you read, write the facts you learn about cattle in the diagram below. You can use this diagram as a summary of your reading.

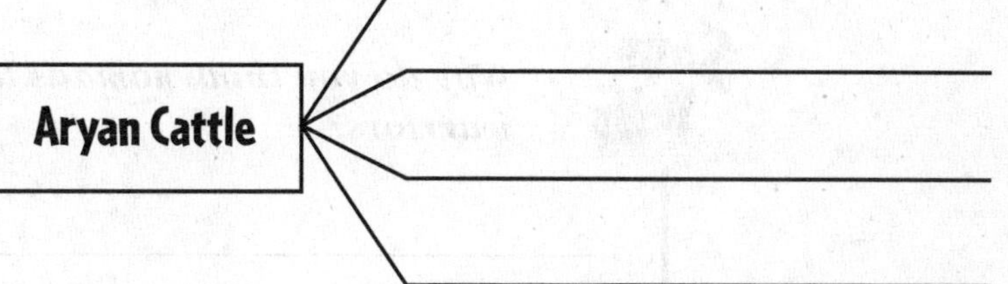

Key Points | Notes

Terms To Know

Define or describe the following terms from this lesson.

Sanskrit

raja

Academic Vocabulary

Define each of these academic vocabulary words from this lesson.

collapse

individual

Terms To Review

Use these terms that you studied earlier in a sentence that reflects the term's meaning.

nomad
(Chapter 1, Section 1)

tribe
(Chapter 3, Section 1)

Sum It Up

Why do you think nomads like the Aryans were great warriors?

Society in Ancient India *(pages 199–201)*

Connecting

The Aryans were light-skinned people and thought they were better than the dark-skinned people they had conquered.

1. Have you ever experienced discrimination because of how you looked or what you believed? How did it feel?

2. Where do you see discrimination in your world today? What effect do you think it has on society?

Terms To Know

Define or describe the following terms from this lesson.

caste

guru

Sum It Up *What were the five major groups in Indian society?*

Section Wrap-up *Now that you have read the section, write the answers to the questions that were included in* **Setting a Purpose for Reading** *at the beginning of the lesson.*

What factors influenced the rise of India's first civilization?

How did the Aryans change life in India?

Chapter 6, Section 2
Hinduism and Buddhism

(Pages 202–208)

Main Idea

Setting a Purpose for Reading Think about these questions as you read:

- What is Hinduism?
- What is Buddhism?

Reading Strategy

As you read pages 203–204 in your textbook, complete the web diagram to identify the major beliefs of Hinduism.

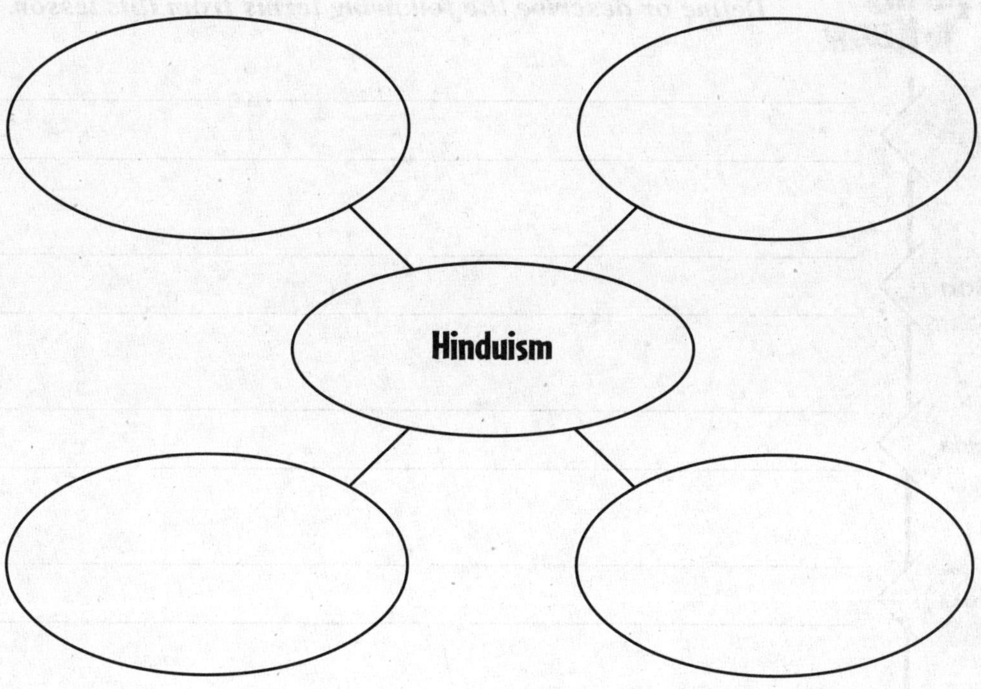

Key Points

Hinduism *(pages 203–204)*

Synthesizing

You are a Hindu servant living in ancient India. Your friend who is not a Hindu has asked you to share about your beliefs. Write a brief paragraph telling your friend what you believe and why your beliefs give you hope in life.

Terms To Know

Define or describe the following terms from this lesson.

Hinduism

reincarnation

dharma

karma

Academic Vocabulary

Define each of these academic vocabulary words from this lesson.

affect

require

Terms To Review

Use each of these terms that you studied earlier in a sentence that reflects the term's meaning.

epic
(Chapter 5, Section 1)

Sanskrit
(Chapter 6, Section 1)

Sum It Up

How is karma related to reincarnation?

Buddhism *(pages 205–208)*

Scanning

Glance quickly over the reading to find answers to the following questions.

1. Who is the Buddha?

2. What is nirvana?

3. What are some of the key beliefs of Buddhism?

Notes

4. What are the different types of Buddhism?

5. Who is the Dalai Lama?

Terms To Know

Define or describe the following terms from this lesson.

Buddhism

nirvana

theocracy

Academic Vocabulary

Define each of these academic vocabulary words from this lesson.

area

aware

Sum It Up

How could a Buddhist reach nirvana?

Now that you have read the section, write the answers to the questions that were included in* Setting a Purpose for Reading *at the beginning of the lesson.

What is Hinduism?

What is Buddhism?

Chapter 6, Section 3
India's First Empires

(Pages 209–216)

Main Idea

Setting a Purpose for Reading Think about these questions as you read:

- What were India's first great empires?
- What contributions did these empires make?

Reading Strategy

As you read pages 210–211 in your textbook, complete this chart to identify the important dates, capital city, and government of the Mauryan Empire.

	Mauryan Empire
Dates	
Capital City	
Government	

The Mauryan Dynasty *(pages 210–211)*

Inferring

Why do many historians think the Mauryan's greatest king was Asoka? Look for facts in your reading that support this statement. Write the facts you find in the diagram below.

King Asoka

Terms To Know

Define or describe these terms from this lesson.

dynasty

stupa

Places To Locate

Briefly describe the following place.

Pataliputra

People To Meet

Explain why this person is important.

Chandragupta Maurya

Academic Vocabulary

Define each of these academic vocabulary words from this lesson.

founded

Key Points | Notes

series

Sum It Up

Why was Asoka an important ruler?

The Gupta Empire *(page 213)*

Determining the Main Idea

As you read, write the main idea of the passage. Review your statement when you have finished reading and revise as needed.

Terms To Know

Define or describe the following term from this lesson.

pilgrim

Academic Vocabulary

Define each of these academic vocabulary words from this lesson.

expand

dominate

Sum It Up *How did the Gupta empire become wealthy?*

Indian Literature and Science (pages 214–216)

Reviewing *As you read, take notes in the chart below. You can use your notes to review the major contributions made by Indians in literature, mathematics, and science.*

Literature	Math	Science

People To Meet *Explain why this person is important.*

Kalidasa

Academic Vocabulary *Define each of these academic vocabulary words from this lesson.*

similar

concept

Terms To Review

Use each of these terms that you studied earlier in a sentence that reflects the term's meaning.

comedy
(Chapter 5, Section 1)

fable
(Chapter 5, Section 1)

Sum It Up

In what branches of science did ancient Indians make advances?

Section Wrap-up

Now that you have read the section, write the answers to the questions that were included in* Setting a Purpose for Reading *at the beginning of the lesson.

What were India's first great empires?

What contributions did these empires make?

Chapter 7, Section 1
China's First Civilizations

(Pages 224–231)

Main Idea

Setting a Purpose for Reading Think about these questions as you read:

- What factors influenced the rise of China's first civilization?
- Why were China's early rulers so powerful?

Reading Strategy

As you read pages 226–231 in your textbook, complete this chart describing the characteristics of the Shang and Zhou dynasties.

	Shang Dynasty	Zhou Dynasty
Dates		
Leadership		
Accomplishments		

Key Points  Notes

China's Geography *(pages 225–226)*

Monitoring Comprehension

How did geography shape China's civilization? Complete the cause-and-effect diagram below to show the impact of geography. Completing the diagram will help you clarify your understanding.

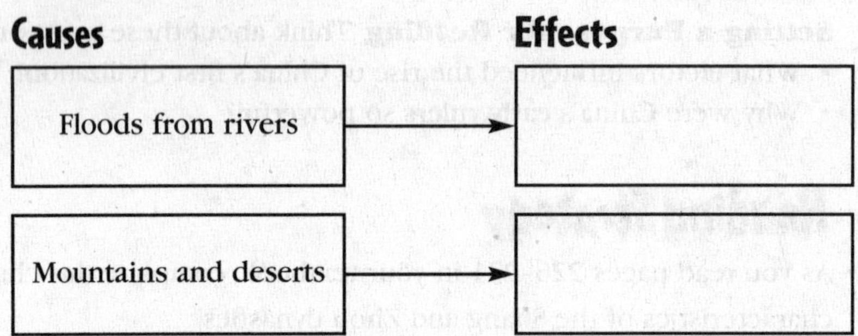

Places To Locate

Briefly describe the following places.

Huang He

____

Chang Jiang

____

Sum It Up

Name two rivers important to early Chinese civilizations.

____

The Shang Dynasty *(pages 226–229)*

Outlining

Complete this outline as you read.

I. Who Were the Shang?

A. ______________________________

B. ______________________________

C. ______________________________

D. ______________________________

II. Spirits and Ancestors

A. ______________________________

B. ______________________________

III. Telling the Future

A. ______________________________

B. ______________________________

IV. The Chinese Language

A. ______________________________

B. ______________________________

V. Shang Artists

A. ______________________________

B. ______________________________

Terms To Know

Define or describe the following terms from this lesson.

dynasty ______________________________

aristocrat ______________________________

pictograph ______________________________

ideograph ______________________________

Notes

Places To Locate

Briefly describe the following place.

Anyang

Academic Vocabulary

Define these academic vocabulary words from this lesson.

recover

interpret

Terms To Review

Use each of these terms that you studied earlier in a sentence that reflects the term's meaning.

artifact
(Chapter 1, Section 1)

oracle
(Chapter 5, Section 1)

Sum It Up

What was the role of the Shang warlords?

The Zhou Dynasty *(pages 229–231)*

Questioning

As you read, write three questions about the main ideas presented in the text. After you have finished reading, write the answers to these questions.

1. ____________________

2. ____________________

3. ____________________

Terms To Know

Define or describe the following terms from this lesson.

bureaucracy ____________________

mandate ____________________

Dao ____________________

Notes

People To Meet

Explain why this person is important.

Wu Wang

Academic Vocabulary

Define these academic vocabulary words from this lesson.

link

item

Terms To Review

Use this term that you studied earlier in a sentence that reflects the term's meaning.

irrigation
(Chapter 1, Section 1)

Sum It Up

What was the chief duty of Chinese kings?

Now that you have read the section, write the answers to the questions that were included in* Setting a Purpose for Reading *at the beginning of the lesson.

What factors influenced the rise of China's first civilization?

Why were China's early rulers so powerful?

Chapter 7, Section 2
Life in Ancient China
(Pages 232–239)

Main Idea

Setting a Purpose for Reading Think about these questions as you read:

- How was Chinese society organized?
- What were the three main Chinese philosophies of the time?

Reading Strategy

As you read pages 233–235 in your textbook, complete the pyramid diagram to show the social classes in ancient China from most important (top) to least important (bottom).

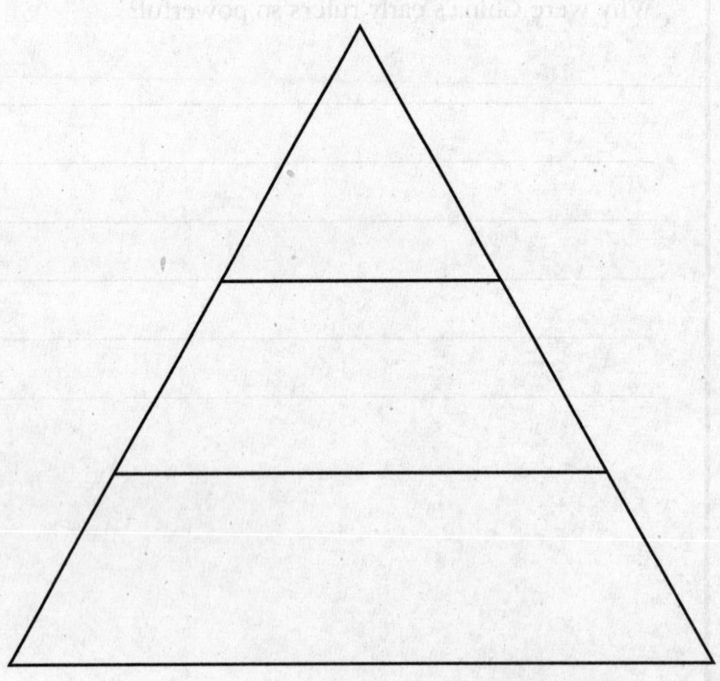

Key Points

Notes

Life in Ancient China *(pages 233–235)*

Skimming

In Chinese society, farmers ranked above merchants. Before you read, skim the passage. Make a note of any points that support this statement. Then, after you read, go back and fill in additional information about the life of farmers in ancient China.

Terms To Know

Define or describe the following terms from this lesson.

social class

filial piety

Academic Vocabulary

Define these academic vocabulary words from this lesson.

rely

convince

Sum It Up

Why did the amount of land owned by each aristocrat decrease over time?

Chinese Thinkers *(pages 235–239)*

Summarizing

As you read, summarize the main points of each of these Chinese philosophers in a few sentences.

Confucius	
Laozi	
Hanfeizi	

Terms To Know

Define or describe the following terms from this lesson.

Confucianism

Daoism

Legalism

Academic Vocabulary

Define these academic vocabulary words from this lesson.

theory

promote

Sum It Up

Why did Hanfeizi believe that people needed laws and punishments?

Section Wrap-up

Now that you have read the section, write the answers to the questions that were included in* Setting a Purpose for Reading *at the beginning of the lesson.

How was Chinese society organized?

What were the three main Chinese philosophies of the time?

Chapter 7, Section 3
The Qin and Han Dynasties

(Pages 240–248)

Main Idea

Setting a Purpose for Reading Think about these questions as you read:

- How did Qin Shihuangdi unify and defend China?
- What developments during the Han dynasty improved life for all Chinese?

Reading Strategy

As you read pages 244–248 in your textbook, complete this diagram to show the inventions of the Han dynasty and the resulting impact on society.

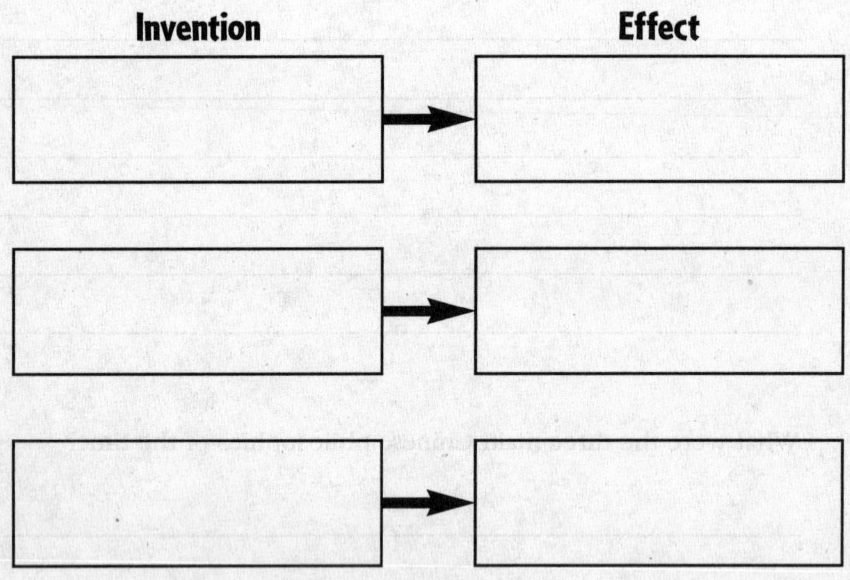

Emperor Qin Shihuangdi *(pages 241–242)*

Evaluating

List the accomplishments of Emperor Qin in the diagram below. Then evaluate his leadership. Write a brief paragraph to answer this question: Was he a good leader? Why or why not?

Qin's Accomplishments

Evaluation

Academic Vocabulary

Define these academic vocabulary words from this lesson.

currency

civil

Sum It Up

Why did Qin face little opposition during most of his reign?

The Han Dynasty *(pages 244–246)*

Monitoring Comprehension

As you read, answer these questions to be sure you understand the main ideas of the section.

1. What effect did the civil service examinations used by the Han dynasty have on the government?

2. Why did the aristocrats gain so much land?

3. What was the effect of the rudder?

Terms To Know

Define or describe the following term from this lesson.

acupuncture

Academic Vocabulary

Define these academic vocabulary words from this lesson.

founded

secure

Notes

Terms To Review

Use each of these terms that you studied earlier in a sentence that reflects the term's meaning.

bureaucracy
(Chapter 7, Section 1)

aristocrats
(Chapter 7, Section 1)

Sum It Up

How did China's empire increase in size during the Han dynasty?

The Silk Road *(pages 246–247)*

Determining the Main Idea

As you read, write the main idea of the passage. Review your statement when you have finished reading and revise as needed.

Sum It Up

Why were only expensive goods carried on the Silk Road?

Key Points

Notes

Major Changes in China *(page 248)*

Skimming

Quickly look over the entire selection to get a general idea about the reading. Then briefly describe the major changes that happened in China during this period.

Terms To Review

Use this term that you studied earlier in a sentence that reflects the term's meaning.

Buddhism
(Chapter 6, Section 2)

Sum It Up

What groups in China were first to adopt Buddhism?

Section Wrap-up

Now that you have read the section, write the answers to the questions that were included in* Setting a Purpose for Reading *at the beginning of the lesson.

How did Qin Shihuangdi unify and defend China?

What developments during the Han dynasty improved life for all Chinese?

Chapter 8, Section 1
Rome's Beginnings
(Pages 262–267)

Main Idea

Setting a Purpose for Reading Think about these questions as you read:
- How did geography play a role in the rise of Roman civilization?
- How did the Romans build Rome from a small city into a great power?

Reading Strategy

As you read pages 263–265 in your textbook, complete this diagram to show how the Etruscans affected the development of Rome.

Etruscans

The Origins of Rome *(pages 263–265)*

Summarizing

Two different legends describe how Rome began. As you read, take notes on these two legends. Then write a two or three sentence summary of each legend.

Romulus and Remus

The *Aeneid*

People To Meet

Explain why these people are important.

Latins

Etruscans

Places To Locate

Briefly describe the following places.

Sicily

Apennines

Latium

Tiber River

Etruria

Academic Vocabulary

Define these academic vocabulary words from this lesson.

isolate

capacity

Terms To Review

Use each of these terms that you studied earlier in a sentence that reflects the term's meaning.

peninsula
(Chapter 4, Section 1)

epic
(Chapter 5, Section 1)

Sum It Up

How did geography help the Romans prosper?

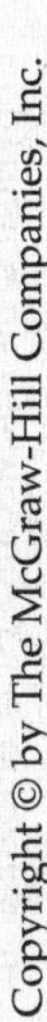

The Birth of a Republic *(pages 265–267)*

Reviewing

What made Rome so strong? As you read, complete the diagram below. Use this diagram to review your learning.

Rome's Strength

Terms To Know

Define or describe the following terms from this lesson.

republic

legion

People To Meet

Explain why this person is important.

Tarquins

Academic Vocabulary

Define these academic vocabulary words from this lesson.

expand

chapter

status

Sum It Up *How did Rome rule its new conquests?*

Section Wrap-up ***Now that you have read the section, write the answers to the questions that were included in* Setting a Purpose for Reading *at the beginning of the lesson.***

How did geography play a role in the rise of Roman civilization?

How did the Romans build Rome from a small city into a great power?

Chapter 8, Section 2
The Roman Republic

(Pages 268–276)

Main Idea

Setting a Purpose for Reading Think about these questions as you read:

- How did Rome's government change?
- How did Rome gain control of the Mediterranean region?

Reading Strategy

As you read pages 269–271 in your textbook, complete this chart listing the government officials and legislative bodies of the Roman Republic.

Officials	Legislative Bodies

Rome's Government *(pages 269–273)*

Questioning

Before you read, scan the reading. Write a question for each section of the lesson. Then after you read, write the answers to your questions.

I. Rome's Government

II. How Did Rome's Government Work?

III. Plebeians Against Patricians

IV. Who Was Cincinnatus?

V. Roman Law

Terms To Know

Define or describe the following terms from this lesson.

patrician

plebeian

Key Points

Notes

consul

veto

praetor

dictator

Academic Vocabulary

Define these academic vocabulary words from this lesson.

reject

interpret

Sum It Up

Before 471 B.C., what right did patricians have that plebeians did not?

Rome Expands *(pages 274–276)*

Sequencing

As you read, number the following events in the correct order.

1. ____ Hannibal attacks Rome
2. ____ Romans lose the Battle of Cannae
3. ____ Scipio's troops defeat the Carthaginians
4. ____ First Punic War begins
5. ____ Rome crushes Carthage's navy off the coast of Sicily
6. ____ Carthage expands its empire into southern Spain
7. ____ Rome gains its first province in Asia
8. ____ Scipio invades Carthage
9. ____ Macedonia comes under Roman rule

Places To Locate

Briefly describe the following places.

Carthage

____

____

Cannae

____

____

Zama

____

____

Notes

People To Meet

Explain why these people are important.

Hannibal

Scipio

Academic Vocabulary

Define these academic vocabulary words from this lesson.

challenge

expand

Sum It Up

How did Rome punish Carthage at the end of the Third Punic War?

Now that you have read the section, write the answers to the questions that were included in* Setting a Purpose for Reading *at the beginning of the lesson.

How did Rome's government change?

How did Rome gain control of the Mediterranean region?

Chapter 8, Section 3
The Fall of the Republic

(Pages 277–283)

Main Idea

Setting a Purpose for Reading Think about these questions as you read:

- What impact did Julius Caesar have on Rome?
- Why did the Roman Republic become an empire under Augustus?

Reading Strategy

As you read pages 278–283 in your textbook, complete this chart to identify the main ideas of Section 3 and supporting details.

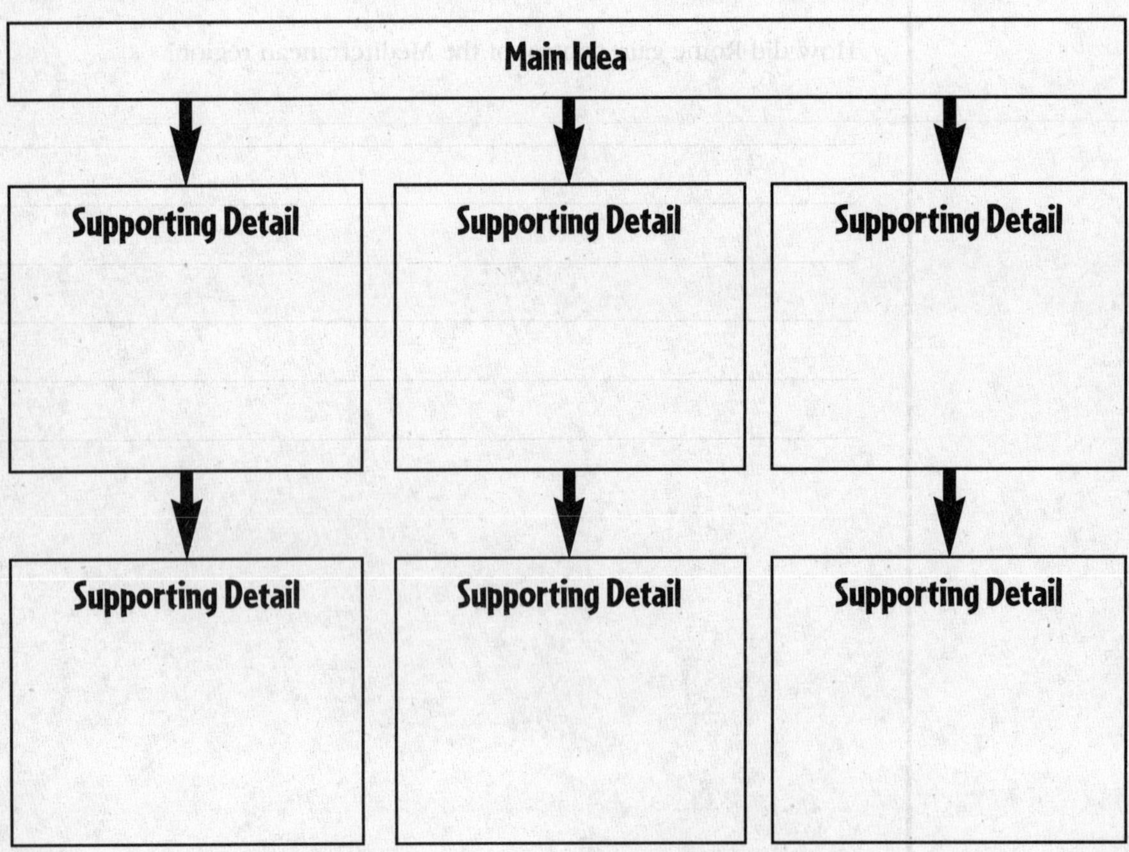

Trouble in the Republic *(pages 278–279)*

Monitoring Comprehension

What factors worked together to weaken the republic? Complete the diagram below to identify the main factors.

Trouble in the Republic

Terms To Know

Define or describe the following term from this lesson.

latifundia

Academic Vocabulary

Define these academic vocabulary words from this lesson.

despite

estate

Sum It Up

What change did Marius make to the Roman army?

Julius Caesar *(pages 280–281)*

Drawing Conclusions

As you read, list the accomplishments, actions, and reforms of Julius Caesar. Then, after you have read the passage, write a general statement about Caesar. Your list of accomplishments and reforms should support your statement.

Accomplishments, Actions, and Reforms:

Conclusion

Terms To Know

Define or describe the following term from this lesson.

triumvirate

Places To Locate

Briefly describe the following place.

Rubicon

Academic Vocabulary ***Define these academic vocabulary words from this lesson.***

tradition

grant

Sum It Up ***Why did Brutus, Cassius, and others kill Caesar?***

Rome Becomes an Empire *(pages 282–283)*

Connecting ***How did the ideas of Cicero affect the writers of the U.S. Constitution? How do these ideas affect your life today? As you read, list the ideas that influenced the founders of our country. The write a brief paragraph about the impact these values have on you today.***

Cicero's Ideas:

How These Ideas Affect Me Today:

Notes

Places To Locate

Briefly describe the following place.

Actium

People To Meet

Explain why each of these people is important.

Octavian

Antony

Cicero

Augustus

Academic Vocabulary

Define these academic vocabulary words from this lesson.

sole

foundation

Sum It Up *How did Octavian's government reflect the ideas of Cicero?*

Section Wrap-up ***Now that you have read the section, write the answers to the questions that were included in* Setting a Purpose for Reading *at the beginning of the lesson.***

What impact did Julius Caesar have on Rome?

Why did the Roman Republic become an empire under Augustus?

Chapter 8, Section 4
The Early Empire

(Pages 286–294)

Main Idea

Setting a Purpose for Reading Think about these questions as you read:

- How did Augustus create a new era of prosperity?
- What changes made the empire rich and prosperous?

Reading Strategy

As you read pages 287–288 in your textbook, complete this chart to show the changes Augustus made in the Roman Empire and the effect of each change.

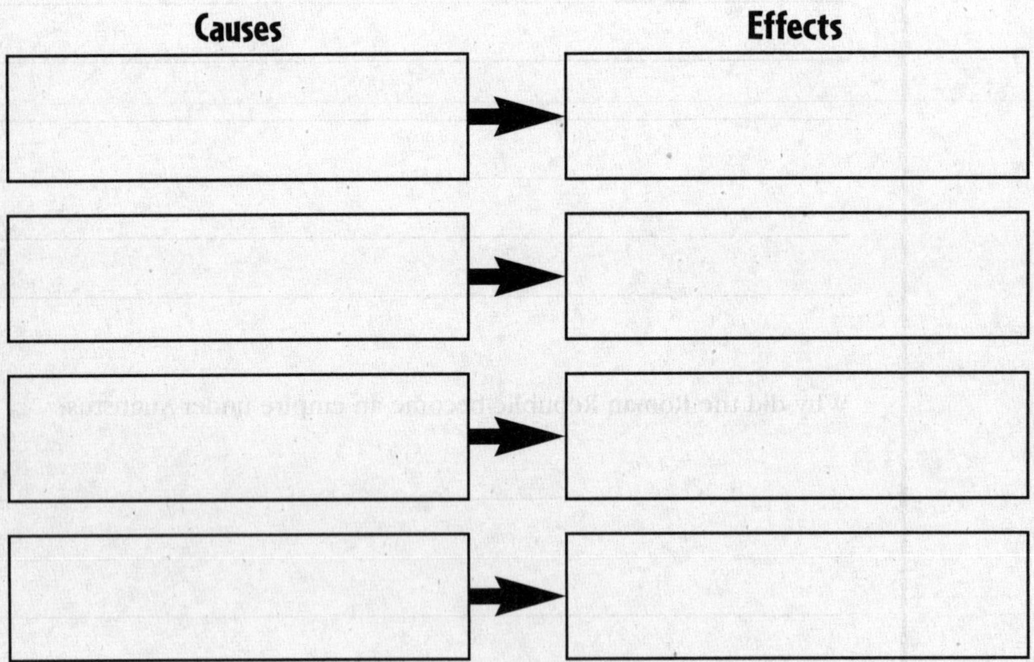

The Emperor Augustus *(pages 287–288)*

Drawing Conclusions

Augustus paved the way for 200 years of peace and prosperity. Why do you think the Roman Empire remained at peace even with weak emperors such as Caligula and Nero?

Terms To Know

Define or describe the following term from this lesson.

Pax Romana

People To Meet

Explain why these people are important.

Caligula

Nero

Academic Vocabulary

Define these academic vocabulary words from this lesson.

conflict

successor

Sum It Up

What did Augustus do to make the empire safer and stronger?

____

____

____

Unity and Prosperity *(pages 290–294)*

Outlining

Complete this outline as you read.

I. Unity and Prosperity

A. ______________________________

B. ______________________________

II. The "Good Emperors"

A. ______________________________

B. ______________________________

III. A Unified Empire

A. ______________________________

B. ______________________________

IV. A Booming Economy

A. ______________________________

B. ______________________________

V. Roads and Money

A. ______________________________

B. ______________________________

VI. Ongoing Inequality

A. ______________________________

Terms To Know

Define or describe the following terms from this lesson.

aqueduct

currency

Places To Locate

Briefly describe the following places.

Rhine River

Danube River

Puteoli

Ostia

Academic Vocabulary

Define these academic vocabulary words from this lesson.

commit

capable

Notes

Sum It Up

Who were the "Good Emperors," and what did they accomplish?

Section Wrap-up

Now that you have read the section, write the answers to the questions that were included in* Setting a Purpose for Reading *at the beginning of the lesson.

How did Augustus create a new era of prosperity?

What changes made the empire rich and prosperous?

Chapter 9, Section 1
Life in Ancient Rome

(Pages 302–310)

Main Idea

Setting a Purpose for Reading Think about these questions as you read:

- How did Roman culture develop and change?
- What was life like in the Roman Empire?

Reading Strategy

As you read pages 306–310 in your textbook, complete this Venn diagram to show similarities and differences between the rich and the poor in Rome.

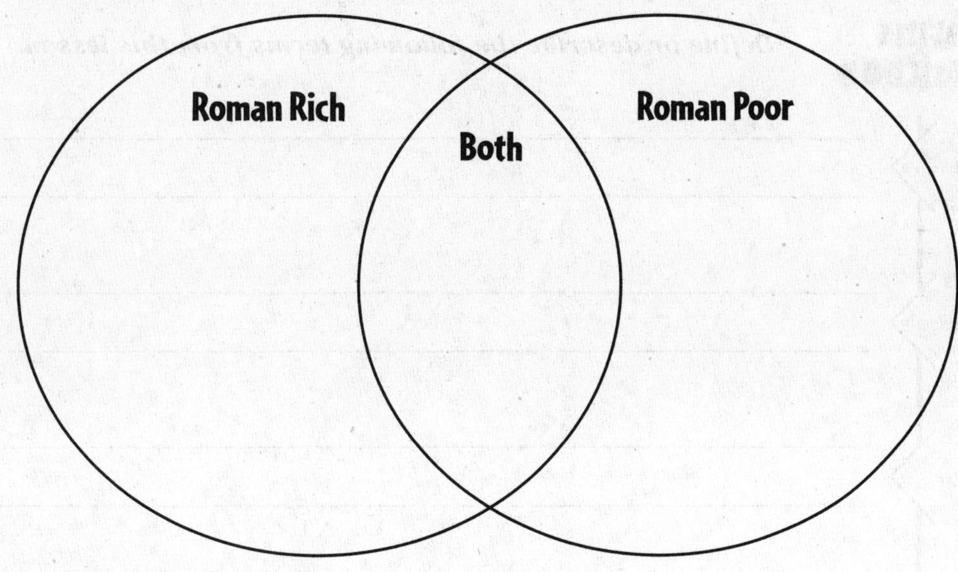

Key Points

Notes

Roman Culture *(pages 303–305)*

Synthesizing

Roman historians took different views of the Roman Empire. After you read the entire passage, read the views of Livy and Tacitus again (page 304). Now you play the historian. Using all you have read and learned about Rome up to this point, write your own view of the empire.

Terms To Know

Define or describe the following terms from this lesson.

vault

satire

ode

anatomy

People To Meet

Explain why these people are important.

Virgil

Horace

Galen

Ptolemy

Academic Vocabulary

Define these academic vocabulary words from this lesson.

feature

technique

Terms To Review

Use each of these terms that you studied earlier in a sentence that reflects the term's meaning.

aqueduct
(Chapter 8, Section 4)

myth
(Chapter 5, Section 1)

Sum It Up

How was the character of Aeneas an ideal Roman?

Key Points

Notes

Daily Life in Rome *(pages 306–310)*

Inferring

The Roman government provided "bread and circuses," or free grain and entertainment. Based on your reading, why do you think the government thought this was necessary? Write a brief paragraph answer this question. Support your answer with facts from your reading.

Terms To Know

Define or describe the following terms from this lesson.

Forum

gladiator

paterfamilias

rhetoric

People To Meet

Explain why this person is important.

Spartacus

Academic Vocabulary

Define these academic vocabulary words from this lesson.

contact

constant

Sum It Up

Describe the freedoms of upper-class women that were not available to women of other classes.

Section Wrap-up

Now that you have read the section, write the answers to the questions that were included in* Setting a Purpose for Reading *at the beginning of the lesson.

How did Roman culture develop and change?

What was life like in the Roman Empire?

Chapter 9, Section 2
The Fall of Rome

(Pages 317–326)

Main Idea

Setting a Purpose for Reading Think about these questions as you read:

- Why was the Roman Empire weakened?
- How would our world be different today if the Roman Empire had never existed?

Reading Strategy

As you read pages 318–324 in your textbook, complete the diagram to show the events that led up to the fall of the Western Roman Empire.

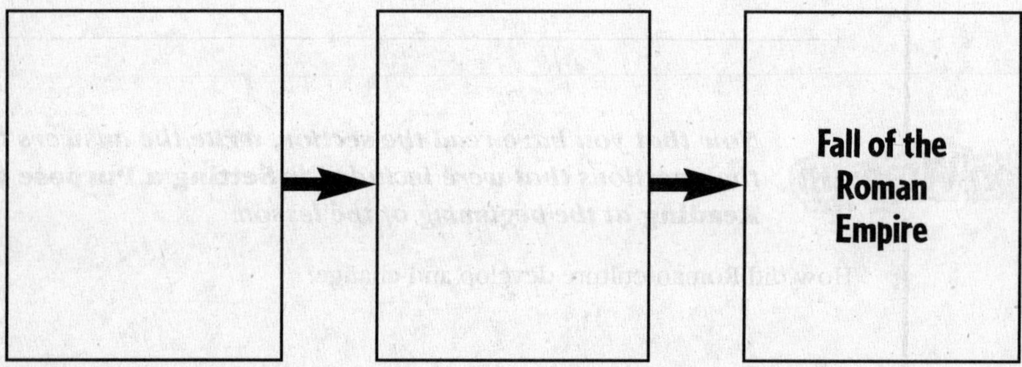

The Decline of Rome *(pages 318–320)*

Summarizing

Use the chart below to summarize the reforms made by Diocletian and Constantine.

Diocletian's Reforms	Constantine's Reforms

Terms To Know

Define or describe the following terms from this lesson.

plague

inflation

barter

reform

Key Points |  **Notes**

Places To Locate

Briefly describe the following place.

Constantinople

Academic Vocabulary

Define these academic vocabulary words from this lesson.

decline

authority

Sum It Up

How did Diocletian try to reverse the decline of Rome?

Rome Falls *(pages 322–324)*

Scanning

Glance quickly over the reading to find answers to the following questions.

1. What happened to the empire in A.D. 395?

2. Why did Germanic groups invade the empire?

3. What happened at the Battle of Adrianople?

4. Who was Alaric?

5. Who was Odoacer?

People To Meet ***Explain why this person is important.***

Theodosius

Sum It Up ***Which event usually marks the fall of the Western Roman Empire?***

Key Points

Notes

The Legacy of Rome *(pages 325–326)*

Reviewing

Use the chart below to take notes on the legacies of Rome. Use your completed chart to review key concepts from your reading.

The Legacy of Rome		
Government	**Culture**	**Religion**

Academic Vocabulary

Define these academic vocabulary words from this lesson.

participate

expand

Terms To Review

Use this term that you studied earlier in a sentence that reflects the term's meaning.

republic
(Chapter 8, Section 1)

Which aspects of the Roman Empire are reflected in present-day cultures?

Section Wrap-up

Now that you have read the section, write the answers to the questions that were included in* Setting a Purpose for Reading *at the beginning of the lesson.

Why was the Roman Empire weakened?

How would our world be different today if the Roman Empire had never existed?

Chapter 9, Section 3
The Byzantine Empire

(Pages 327–334)

Main Idea

Setting a Purpose for Reading Think about these questions as you read:

- What policies and reforms made the Byzantine Empire strong?
- What ideas and beliefs shaped Byzantine culture?

Reading Strategy

As you read pages 328–330 in your textbook, complete this chart to show the causes and effects of Justinian's new law code.

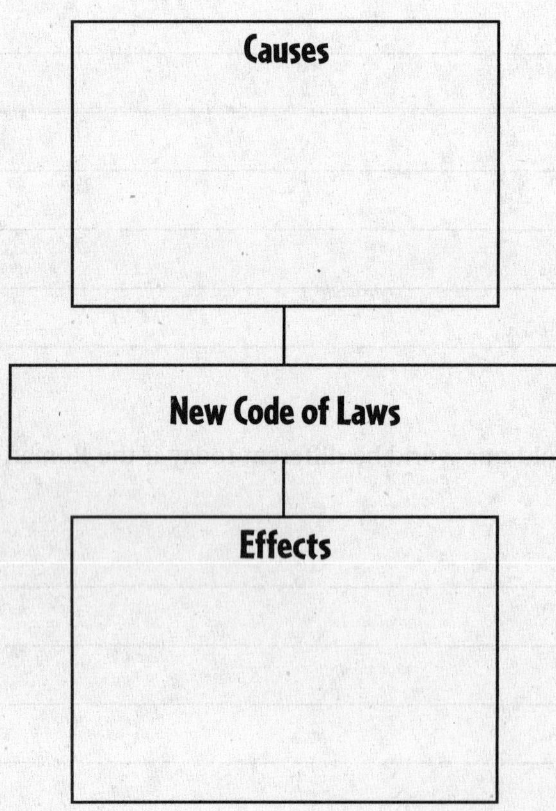

The Rise of the Byzantines *(pages 328–329)*

Previewing

Preview this section to get an idea of what is ahead. First, skim the section. Then write a sentence or two explaining what you think you will be learning. After you have finished reading, revise your statements as necessary.

Places To Locate

Briefly describe the following places.

Black Sea

Aegean Sea

Academic Vocabulary

Define this academic vocabulary word from this lesson.

secure

Terms To Review

Use this term that you studied earlier in a sentence that reflects the term's meaning.

peninsula
(Chapter 4, Section 1)

Why did the Byzantine Empire have such a blending of cultures?

Emperor Justinian *(pages 329–330)*

Determining the Main Idea

As you read, write the main idea of the passage. Review your statement when you have finished reading and revise as needed.

People To Meet ***Explain why these people are important.***

Justinian

Theodora

Belisarius

Tribonian

Academic Vocabulary ***Define these academic vocabulary words from this lesson.***

income

rely

Sum It Up ***What did Justinian accomplish during his reign?***

Byzantine Civilization *(pages 332–334)*

Outlining

Complete this outline as you read.

I. The Importance of Trade

A. ______

B. ______

II. Byzantine Art and Architecture

A. ______

B. ______

III. Byzantine Women

A. ______

B. ______

IV. Byzantine Education

A. ______

B. ______

Terms To Know

Define or describe the following terms from this lesson.

mosaic ______

saint ______

regent ______

Academic Vocabulary

Define this academic vocabulary word from this lesson.

enormous

Terms To Review

Use this term that you studied earlier in a sentence that reflects the term's meaning.

caravan
(Chapter 1, Section 3)

Sum It Up

What church was the religious center of the Byzantine Empire?

Now that you have read the section, write the answers to the questions that were included in* Setting a Purpose for Reading *at the beginning of the lesson.

What policies and reforms made the Byzantine Empire strong?

What ideas and beliefs shaped Byzantine culture?

Chapter 10, Section 1

The First Christians

(Pages 342–350)

Main Idea

Setting a Purpose for Reading Think about these questions as you read:

- What did Jesus teach?
- How did people react to his teachings?

Reading Strategy

As you read pages 348–350 in your textbook, complete this diagram to show the purposes of the early Christian churches.

Purposes of Churches

Key Points

Notes

The Jews and the Romans *(page 343)*

Connecting

The Jews responded in different ways to Roman rule. Some worked with the Romans. Some followed their own traditions more closely. Some moved away. Others rebelled. How do you feel when someone else—maybe a parent, teacher, peer, or other leader—is in control of your life? How do you respond when this person shares your values and beliefs? How do you respond when they do not? Write a brief paragraph answering these questions.

Places To Locate

Briefly describe the following places.

Jerusalem

Judaea

Academic Vocabulary

Define these academic vocabulary words from this lesson.

convince

community

Sum It Up

Why did many Jews leave Judaea after the A.D. 132 revolt?

The Life of Jesus *(pages 344–347)*

Responding

This section states that Jesus taught in parables. The parable of the Good Samaritan is one of the best known parables. As you read that parable, consider your personal response to it. Also consider why Jesus presented his teachings in the form of a parable. Write your response in a brief paragraph.

Terms To Know

Define or describe the following terms from this lesson.

messiah

disciple

parable

resurrection

Places To Locate

Briefly describe the following places.

Jerusalem

Nazareth

Galilee

Academic Vocabulary

Define these academic vocabulary words from this lesson.

decade

assemble

Terms To Review

Use this term that you studied earlier in a sentence that reflects the term's meaning.

prophet
(Chapter 2, Section 2)

Sum It Up

What were the main ideas Jesus taught during his life?

The First Christians *(pages 348–350)*

Predicting

On the chart below, write headings that indicate the kind of information you expect to find in the reading. Use the Main Idea, Reading Focus, main headings, and terms to help you with the headings. The first one has been done for you. Then as you read, write details from the text under the correct headings.

Early Christians		

Terms To Know

Define or describe the following terms from this lesson.

apostle

salvation

Academic Vocabulary

Define this academic vocabulary word from this lesson.

reside

Sum It Up

Who were Peter and Paul, and why were they important?

Now that you have read the section, write the answers to the questions that were included in* Setting a Purpose for Reading *at the beginning of the lesson.

What did Jesus teach?

How did people react to his teachings?

Chapter 10, Section 2
The Christian Church

(Pages 351–356)

Main Idea

Setting a Purpose for Reading Think about these questions as you read:

- How did Christianity become the official religion of the Roman Empire?
- How was the early Christian Church organized?

Reading Strategy

As you read pages 352–354 in your textbook, complete the diagram to show reasons for the growth of Christianity.

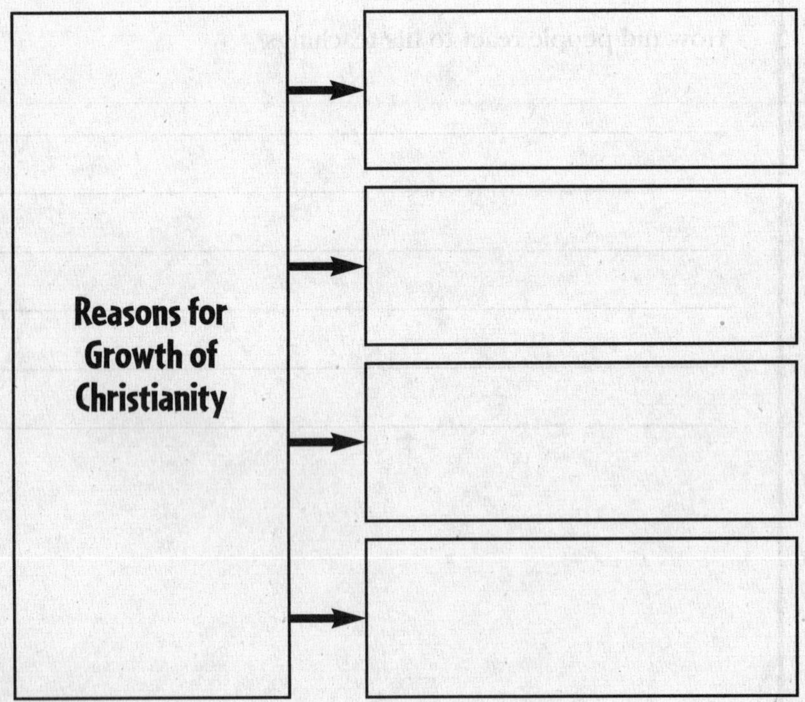

A Growing Faith *(pages 352–354)*

Inferring ***As you read, infer the answer to the following question.***

Why did Christians refuse to serve in the army or hold public office?

Terms To Know ***Define or describe the following terms from this lesson.***

persecute

martyr

People To Meet ***Explain why these people are important.***

Constantine

Helena

Theodosius

Notes

Academic Vocabulary

Define these academic vocabulary words from this lesson.

establish

issue

Sum It Up

Why did the Romans see the Christians as traitors?

The Early Church *(pages 355–356)*

Glance quickly over the reading to find answers to complete the chart below.

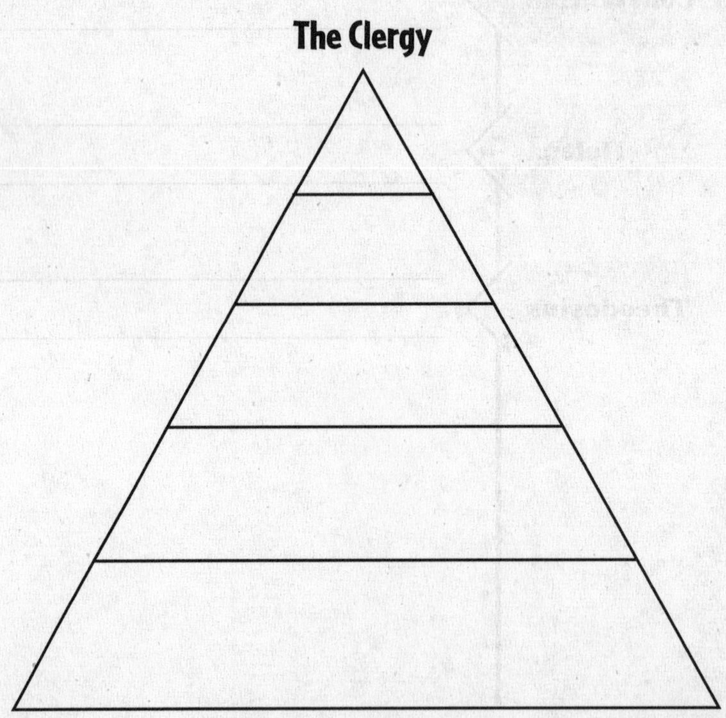

Terms To Know

Define or describe the following terms from this lesson.

hierarchy

clergy

laity

doctrine

gospel

Academic Vocabulary

Define these academic vocabulary words from this lesson.

unify

authority

Sum It Up

What are the Gospels, and why are they significant?

Now that you have read the section, write the answers to the questions that were included in* Setting a Purpose for Reading *at the beginning of the lesson.

How did Christianity become the official religion of the Roman Empire?

How was the early Christian Church organized?

Chapter 10, Section 3
The Spread of Christian Ideas

(Pages 358–364)

Main Idea

Setting a Purpose for Reading Think about these questions as you read:

- How did church and government work together in the Byzantine Empire?
- How did Christian ideas spread to Europe?

Reading Strategy

As you read pages 361–364 in your textbook, complete this diagram to show the reach of Christian missionaries.

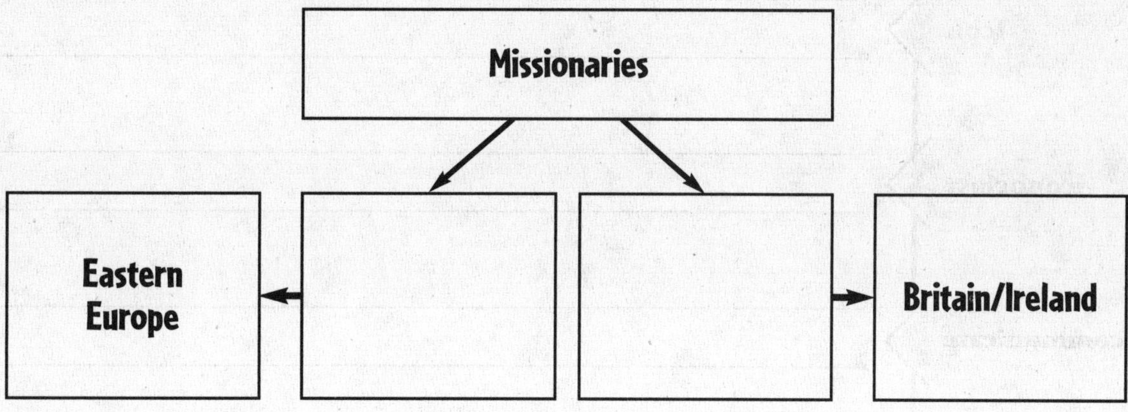

The Byzantine Church *(pages 359–361)*

Summarizing

As you read, look for the reasons for the conflicts that led up to the break between the Roman Catholic and Eastern Orthodox Churches. Then, after you read, use the chart below to summarize the major reasons for the split.

Church Conflicts

Terms To Know

Define or describe the following terms from this lesson.

icon

iconoclast

excommunicate

schism

People To Meet

Explain why this person is important.

Charlemagne

Places To Locate

Briefly describe the following place.

Byzantine Empire

Academic Vocabulary

Define these academic vocabulary words from this lesson.

survive

conflict

Sum It Up

How did the church and government work together in the Byzantine Empire?

Christian Ideas Spread *(pages 361–364)*

Sequencing

As you read, number the following events in the correct order.

1. ____ Patrick brings Christianity to Ireland

2. ____ Cyril invents a new Slavic alphabet

3. ____ Paula builds churches, a hospital, and a convent in Palestine

4. ____ Monks band together into the first monasteries

5. ____ Pope Gregory I sends monks to take Christianity to England

Terms To Know

Define or describe the following terms from this lesson.

monastery ____________________

missionary ____________________

People To Meet

Explain why these people are important.

Basil ____________________

Benedict ____________________

Cyril

Patrick

Places To Locate

Briefly describe the following places.

Britain

Ireland

Sum It Up

How did Christianity spread westward?

Now that you have read the section, write the answers to the questions that were included in* Setting a Purpose for Reading *at the beginning of the lesson.

How did church and government work together in the Byzantine Empire?

How did Christian ideas spread to Europe?

Chapter 11, Section 1
The Rise of Islam
(Pages 372–378)

Main Idea

Setting a Purpose for Reading Think about these questions as you read:

- How did geography shape the Arab way of life?
- What did Muhammad teach?

Reading Strategy

As you read pages 377–378 in your textbook, complete this diagram to identify the Five Pillars of the Islamic faith.

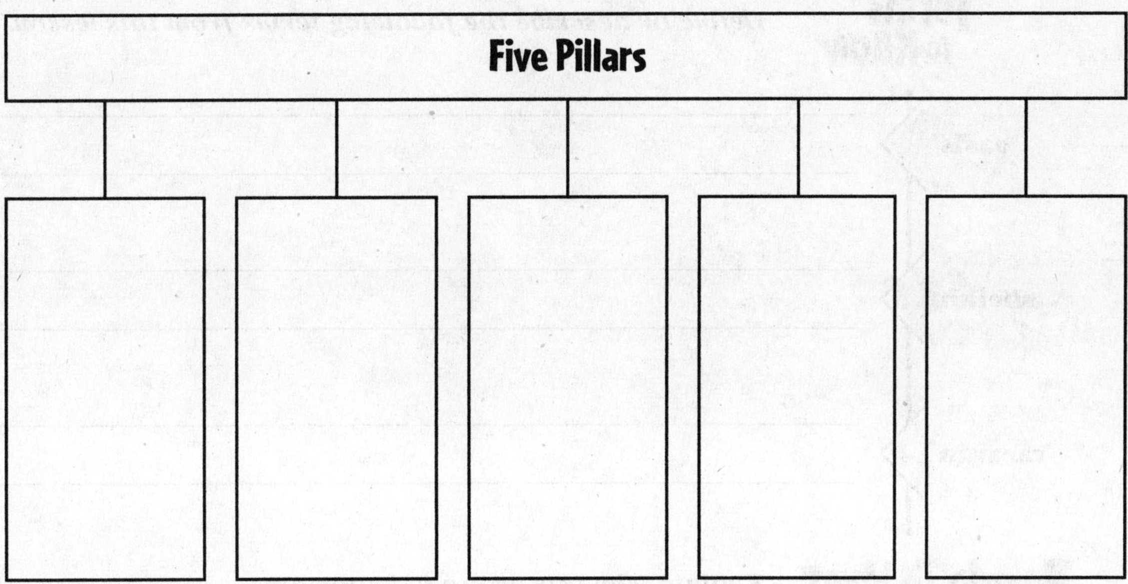

Key Points

Notes

Daily Life in Early Arabia *(pages 373–374)*

Responding

Picture yourself in the deserts of Arabia. The heat is intense. Water is scarce. You live life as a Bedouin, traveling from oasis to oasis. What do you experience in a day? What do you like about your life? What do you not like? After you read the passage, write a paragraph about your life.

Terms To Know

Define or describe the following terms from this lesson.

oasis

sheikh

caravan

People To Meet

Explain why this group is important.

Bedouins

Notes

Places To Locate

Briefly describe the following places.

Makkah

Kaaba

Academic Vocabulary

Define these academic vocabulary words from this lesson.

intense

transport

Sum It Up

How did geography shape life in Arabia?

Muhammad: Islam's Prophet *(pages 374–375)*

Questioning

As you read, write three questions about the main ideas presented in the text. After you have finished reading, write the answers to these questions.

1.

2.

3.

Places To Locate

Briefly describe the following place.

Madinah

Academic Vocabulary

Define these academic vocabulary words from this lesson.

create

require

Terms To Review

Use this term that you studied earlier in a sentence that reflects the term's meaning.

prophet
(Chapter 3, Section 2)

Sum It Up

Why did Muhammad's message appeal to the poor?

Islam's Teachings *(pages 377–378)*

Previewing

Before you read, look over the passage. What do you already know about Islam? What do you want to learn about Islam? Complete the first two columns in the table below. Then, after you read, fill in the third column with new information you learned.

What I know about Islam	What I want to learn about Islam	What I learned about Islam

Terms To Know

Define or describe the following term from this lesson.

Quran

Academic Vocabulary

Define this academic vocabulary word from this lesson.

instruct

Sum It Up

What role do the Quran and Sunna play in Muslim daily life?

Section Wrap-up

Now that you have read the section, write the answers to the questions that were included in **Setting a Purpose for Reading** ***at the beginning of the lesson.***

How did geography shape the Arab way of life?

What did Muhammad teach?

Chapter 11, Section 2
Islamic Empires
(Pages 379–386)

Main Idea

Setting a Purpose for Reading Think about these questions as you read:
- How did Islam spread?
- Why did Muslims split into two groups?

Reading Strategy

As you read pages 380–381 in your textbook, complete the diagram to show why the Arabs were successful conquerors.

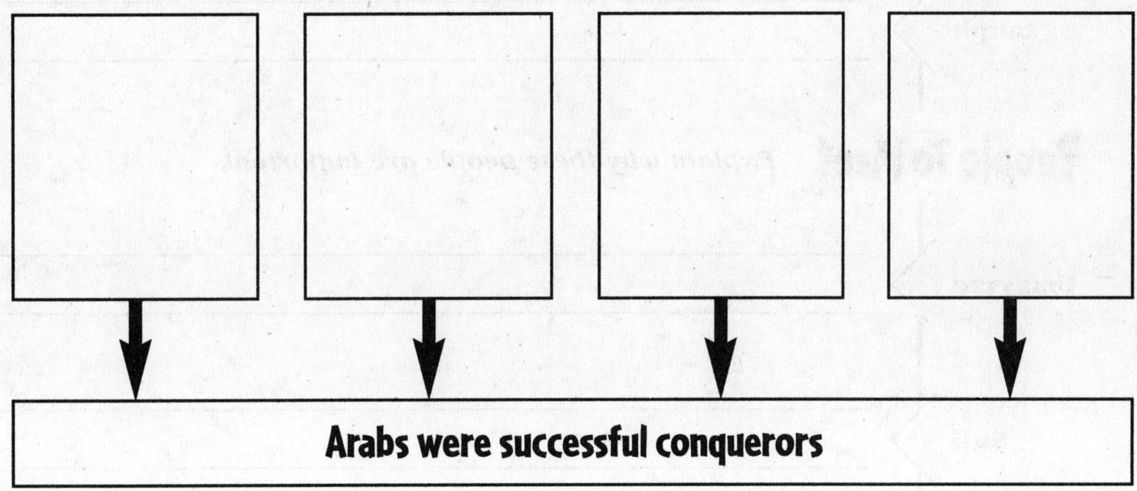

The Spread of Islam *(pages 380–381)*

Determining the Main Idea

As you read, write the main idea of the passage. Review your statement when you have finished reading, and revise as needed.

Terms To Know

Define or describe the following term from this lesson.

caliph

People To Meet

Explain why these people are important.

Umayyad

Sufi

Places To Locate

Briefly describe the following places.

Damascus

Indonesia

Timbuktu

Key Points | Notes

Academic Vocabulary

Define these academic vocabulary words from this lesson.

create

successor

expand

Sum It Up

How did Arabs spread the religion of Islam through trade?

Struggles Within Islam *(pages 382–383)*

Sequencing

As you read, number the following rulers and dynasties in the correct order.

1. ____ Umayyads
2. ____ Muhammad
3. ____ Seljuks
4. ____ Mongols
5. ____ Abbasids

Notes

Terms To Know

Define or describe the following terms from this lesson.

Shiite

Sunni

sultan

People To Meet

Explain why this group is important.

Abbasids

Places To Locate

Briefly describe the following place.

Baghdad

Academic Vocabulary

Define these academic vocabulary words from this lesson.

policy

devote

Sum It Up *What is the difference between Shiite and Sunni Muslims?*

Later Muslim Empires *(pages 384–386)*

Reviewing *As you read, fill in the information in the chart below. Use this chart to review information about the Ottoman and Mogul empires.*

	Ottoman Empire	Mogul Empire
Great leader		
Location		
Capital		
Accomplishments		

People To Meet *Explain why these people are important.*

Suleiman I

Moguls

Akbar

Places To Locate

Briefly describe the following place.

Delhi

Academic Vocabulary

Define these academic vocabulary words from this lesson.

style

impose

Sum It Up

How did Constantinople change in 1453?

Now that you have read the section, write the answers to the questions that were included in* Setting a Purpose for Reading *at the beginning of the lesson.

How did Islam spread?

Why did Muslims split into two groups?

Chapter 11, Section 3
Muslim Ways of Life

(Pages 387–394)

Main Idea

Setting a Purpose for Reading Think about these questions as you read:

- What was Muslim society like?
- How did Muslims contribute to science and culture?

Reading Strategy

As you read pages 388–390 in your textbook, complete this pyramid to show the social classes in the early Muslim world.

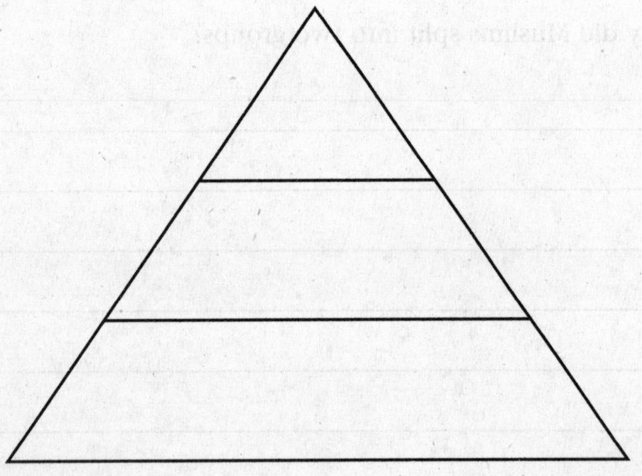

Trade and Everyday Life *(pages 388–390)*

Inferring

Why would language and coins make trade easier for the Muslims? Write your answer in the space below.

Terms To Know

Define or describe the following terms from this lesson.

mosque

bazaar

Academic Vocabulary

Define these academic vocabulary words from this lesson.

similar

widespread

Key Points

Notes

Sum It Up

How did the Muslim rulers give their merchants an advantage?

Muslim Achievements *(pages 390–394)*

Scanning

Before you read, scan the passage looking for information to include in the table below. After your read, add information to complete the table.

Muslim Achievements		
Math and Science	**Writing**	**Art and Buildings**

Terms To Know

Define or describe the following terms from this lesson.

minaret

crier

People To Meet

Explain why these people are important.

Mamun

al-Razi

Ibn Sina

Omar Khayyam

Ibn Khaldun

Places To Locate

Briefly describe the following places.

Granada

Agra

Sum It Up

What contributions did Muslims make in math?

Now that you have read the section, write the answers to the questions that were included in* Setting a Purpose for Reading *at the beginning of the lesson.

What was Muslim society like?

____

____

____

____

____

____

How did Muslims contribute to science and culture?

____

____

____

____

____

____

Chapter 12, Section 1
China Reunites

(Pages 408–415)

Main Idea

Setting a Purpose for Reading Think about these questions as you read:

- How did the Sui and Tang dynasties reunite China?
- What religious ideas influenced China in the Middle Ages?

Reading Strategy

As you read pages 409–412 in your textbook, complete this table to show the time periods, most important rulers, and the reasons for decline of the Sui and Tang dynasties.

	Sui	Tang
Time Period		
Important Rulers		
Reasons for Decline		

Rebuilding China's Empire *(pages 409–412)*

Sequencing

As you read, place the following events in the correct order by numbering them in the spaces provided.

1. ____ Taizong rules

2. ____ The Song dynasty rules

3. ____ Yangdi builds the Grand Canal

4. ____ Wendi reunites China

5. ____ Empress Wu rules

6. ____ The Han empire ends

Terms To Know

Define or describe the following terms from this lesson.

warlord ______________________________

economy ______________________________

reform ______________________________

People To Meet

Explain why these people are important.

Wendi ______________________________

Empress Wu ______________________________

Places To Locate

Briefly describe the following place.

Korea

Academic Vocabulary

Define these academic vocabulary words from this lesson.

route

civil

Terms To Review

Use each of these terms that you studied earlier in a sentence that reflects the term's meaning.

dynasty
(Chapter 7, Section 1)

tribute
(Chapter 3, Section 2)

Sum It Up

How did Wendi unite China?

Key Points

Notes

Buddhism Spreads to China *(pages 412–413)*

Analyzing

Why did Buddhism spread to China and what caused it to decline? After you read, complete the diagram below to analyze the cause-and-effect relationships.

Cause	Effect
	Buddhism spreads to China
	Buddhism declines in China

Terms To Know

Define or describe the following term from this lesson.

monastery

Places To Locate

Briefly describe the following place.

Japan

Terms To Review

Use each of these terms that you studied earlier in a sentence that reflects the term's meaning.

Buddhism (Chapter 6, Section 2)

monastery (Chapter 10, Section 3)

Sum It Up *Why did some Chinese people dislike Buddhism?*

New Confucian Ideas *(pages 413–415)*

Evaluating *As you read, take notes on Neo-Confucianism and the scholar-officials. Use your notes to answer this question: How did Neo-Confucianism help strengthen the government?*

Terms To Review *Use each of these terms that you studied earlier in a sentence that reflects the term's meaning.*

Confucianism
(Chapter 7, Section 2)

bureaucracy
(Chapter 7, Section 1)

Sum It Up *How did Confucianism change in China?*

Now that you have read the section, write the answers to the questions that were included in* Setting a Purpose for Reading *at the beginning of the lesson.

How did the Sui and Tang dynasties reunite China?

What religious ideas influenced China in the Middle Ages?

Chapter 12, Section 2
Chinese Society
(Pages 416–422)

Main Idea

Setting a Purpose for Reading Think about these questions as you read:
- What new technologies developed in China?
- How did art and literature develop in the Tang and Song dynasties?

Reading Strategy

As you read pages 418–420 in your textbook, complete this chart to describe the new technologies developed in China during the Middle Ages.

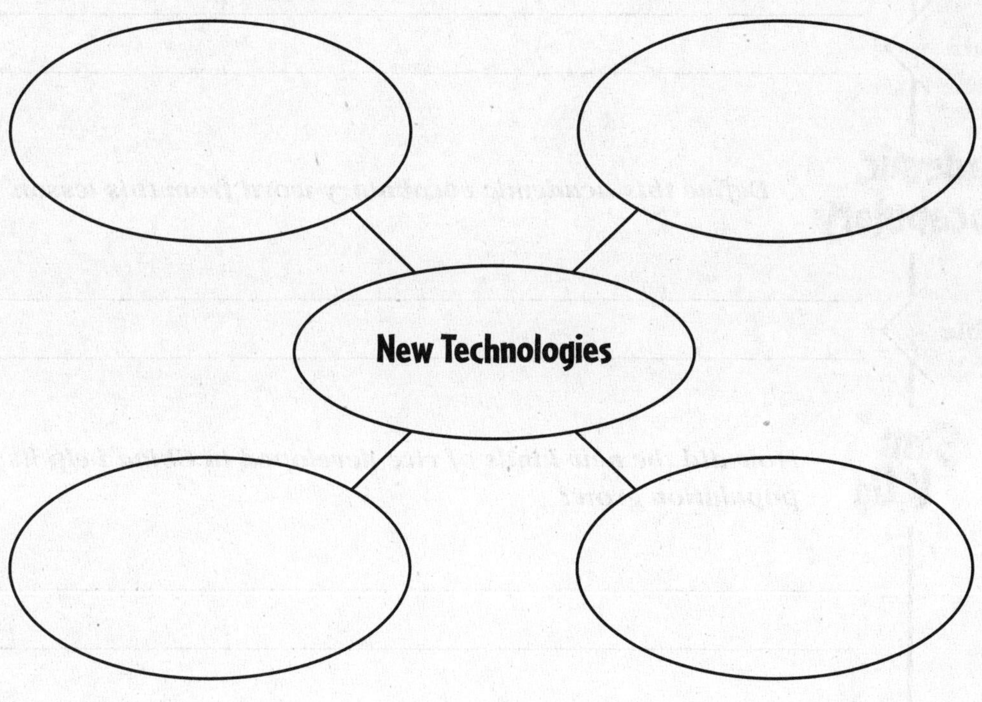

A Growing Economy *(pages 417–418)*

Determining the Main Idea

As you read, write the main idea of the passage. Review your statement when you have finished reading, and revise as needed.

Terms To Know

Define or describe the following term from this lesson.

porcelain

Academic Vocabulary

Define this academic vocabulary word from this lesson.

available

Sum It Up

How did the new kinds of rice developed in China help its population grow?

New Technology *(pages 418–420)*

Inferring

As you read the passage, list the inventions and new technology that would have affected China's military. Then answer this question: How did China's inventions in the Middle Ages strengthen their dynasties?

Academic Vocabulary

Define this academic vocabulary word from this lesson.

method

Terms To Review

Use this term that you studied earlier in a sentence that reflects the term's meaning.

technology
(Chapter 1, Section 1)

Sum It Up

Why was the invention of printing so important?

Key Points

Notes

Art and Literature *(pages 420–422)*

Drawing Conclusions

As you read the information about Chinese art and literature, write a general statement about each art form: poetry, painting, and porcelain.

1. Poetry

2. Painting

3. Porcelain

Terms To Know

Define or describe the following term from this lesson.

calligraphy

Places To Locate

Briefly describe the following place.

Changan

People To Meet

Explain why these people are important.

Li Bo

Du Fu

Sum It Up

What did Du Fu often write about?

Section Wrap-up

Now that you have read the section, write the answers to the questions that were included in* Setting a Purpose for Reading *at the beginning of the lesson.

What new technologies developed in China?

How did art and literature develop in the Tang and Song dynasties?

Chapter 12, Section 3
The Mongols in China

(Pages 423–429)

Main Idea

Setting a Purpose for Reading Think about these questions as you read:

- Who was Genghis Khan?
- How did Mongol rule impact China?

Reading Strategy

As you read pages 424–429 in your textbook, complete this diagram to show the accomplishments of Genghis Khan's reign.

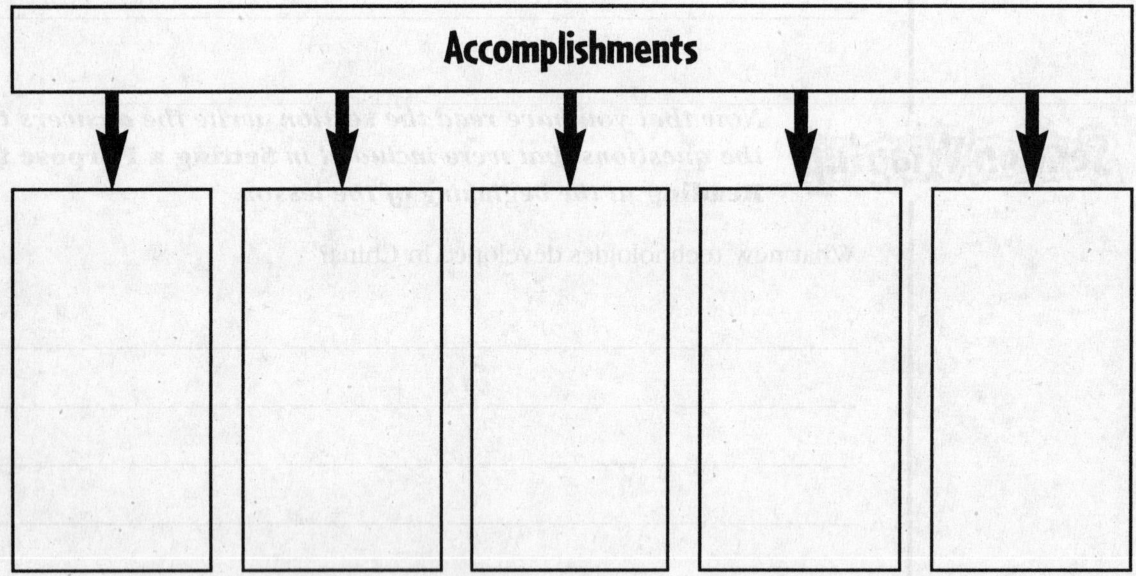

The Mongols *(pages 424–426)*

Scanning

Glance over the reading to find answers to the following questions. After you read, fill in any missing details from the passage.

1. What were the Mongols known for?

2. What were Mongol warriors known for?

3. How big was the Mongol Empire?

Terms To Know

Define or describe the following terms from this lesson.

tribe

steppe

terror

Places To Locate

Briefly describe the following places.

Mongolia

Gobi

Academic Vocabulary

Define these academic vocabulary words from this lesson.

code

encounter

Sum It Up

What military and economic reasons explain why the Mongols were able to build an empire so quickly?

Mongol Rule in China *(pages 428–429)*

Evaluating

As you read, take notes on the actions and effects of Mongol rule in China in the chart below. Then, based on your notes, write a short paragraph evaluating the leadership of Kublai Khan. Use specific examples from your notes to support your opinion.

Mongol Rule in China

Evaluation:

People To Meet

Explain why each of these people is important.

Kublai Khan

Marco Polo

Places To Locate

Briefly describe the following places.

Karakorum

Khanbaliq

Beijing

Sum It Up

Who founded the Yuan dynasty?

Section Wrap-up

Now that you have read the section, write the answers to the questions that were included in* Setting a Purpose for Reading *at the beginning of the lesson.

Who was Genghis Khan?

How did Mongol rule impact China?

Chapter 12, Section 4
The Ming Dynasty
(Pages 430–436)

Main Idea

Setting a Purpose for Reading Think about these questions as you read:

- How did Ming rulers make China's government strong?
- What did the Ming rulers accomplish?

Reading Strategy

As you read pages 433–436 in your textbook, complete this chart to show cause-and-effect links in China's early trade voyages.

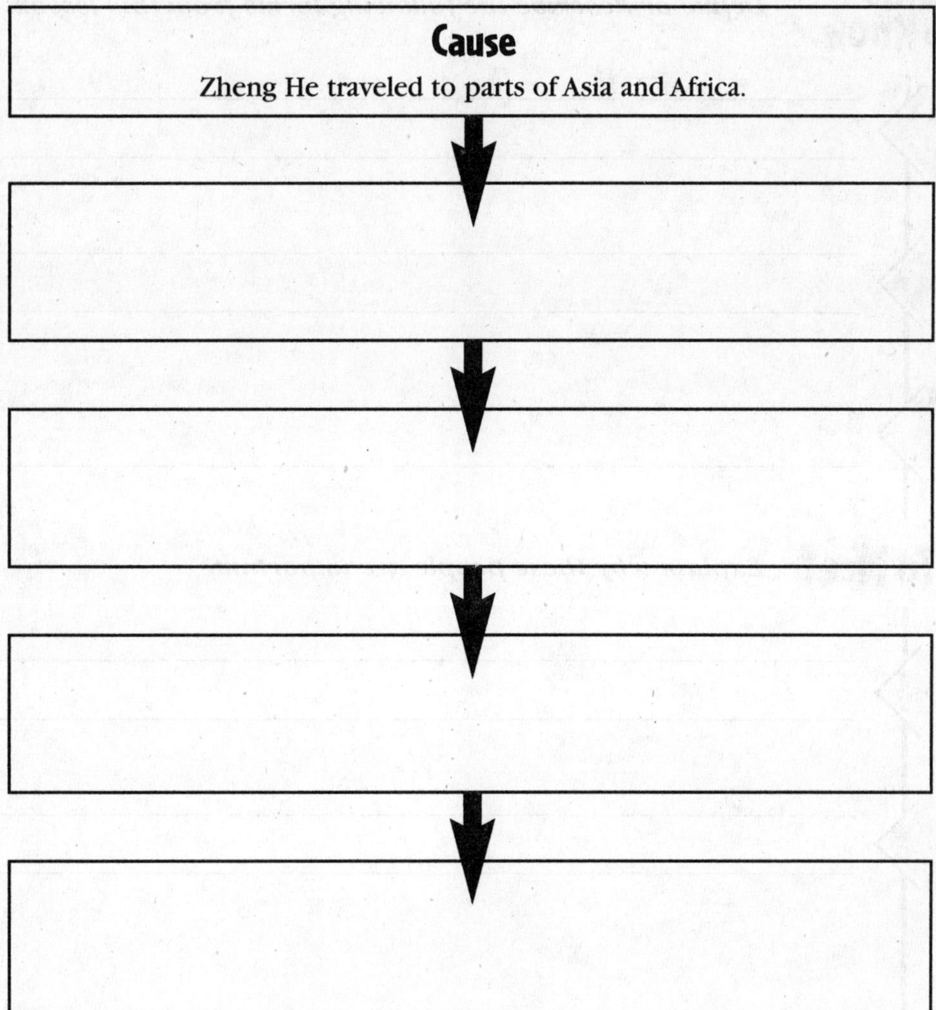

Notes

The Rise of Ming *(pages 431–432)*

Monitoring Comprehension

As you read, list the ways the Ming reformed China in the chart below.

Ming Reforms

Terms To Know

Define or describe the following terms from this lesson.

treason

census

novel

People To Meet

Explain why these people are important.

Zhu Yuanzhang

Yong Le

Places To Locate

Briefly describe the following place.

Nanjing

Academic Vocabulary

Define these academic vocabulary words from this lesson.

accurate

economy

Terms To Review

Use each of these terms that you studied earlier in a sentence that reflects the term's meaning.

reform
(Chapter 9, Section 2)

drama
(Chapter 5, Section 1)

Sum It Up

What was the Forbidden City?

China Explores the World *(pages 433–436)*

Outlining

Complete this outline as you read.

I. Who Was Zheng He?

A. ______________________

B. ______________________

II. Where Did Zheng He Travel?

A. ______________________

B. ______________________

C. ______________________

D. ______________________

III. The Europeans Arrive in China

A. ______________________

B. ______________________

C. ______________________

IV. Why Did the Ming Dynasty Fall?

A. ______________________

B. ______________________

Terms To Know

Define or describe the following term from this section.

barbarian ______________________

____

Places To Locate

Briefly describe the following place.

Portugal

People To Meet

Explain why this person is important.

Zheng He

Terms To Review

Use each of these terms that you studied earlier in a sentence that reflects the term's meaning.

tribute
(Chapter 3, Section 2)

missionary
(Chapter 10, Section 3)

Sum It Up

What caused the Ming dynasty to decline and fall?

Now that you have read the section, write the answers to the questions that were included in* Setting a Purpose for Reading *at the beginning of the lesson.

How did Ming rulers make China's government strong?

What did the Ming rulers accomplish?

Chapter 13, Section 1

The Rise of African Civilizations

(Pages 444–453)

Main Idea

Setting a Purpose for Reading Think about these questions as you read:

- How did geography affect the development of African kingdoms?
- What factors contributed to the growth of African civilizations?

Reading Strategy

As you read pages 448–449 in your textbook, complete these diagrams describing the accomplishments of the West African empires.

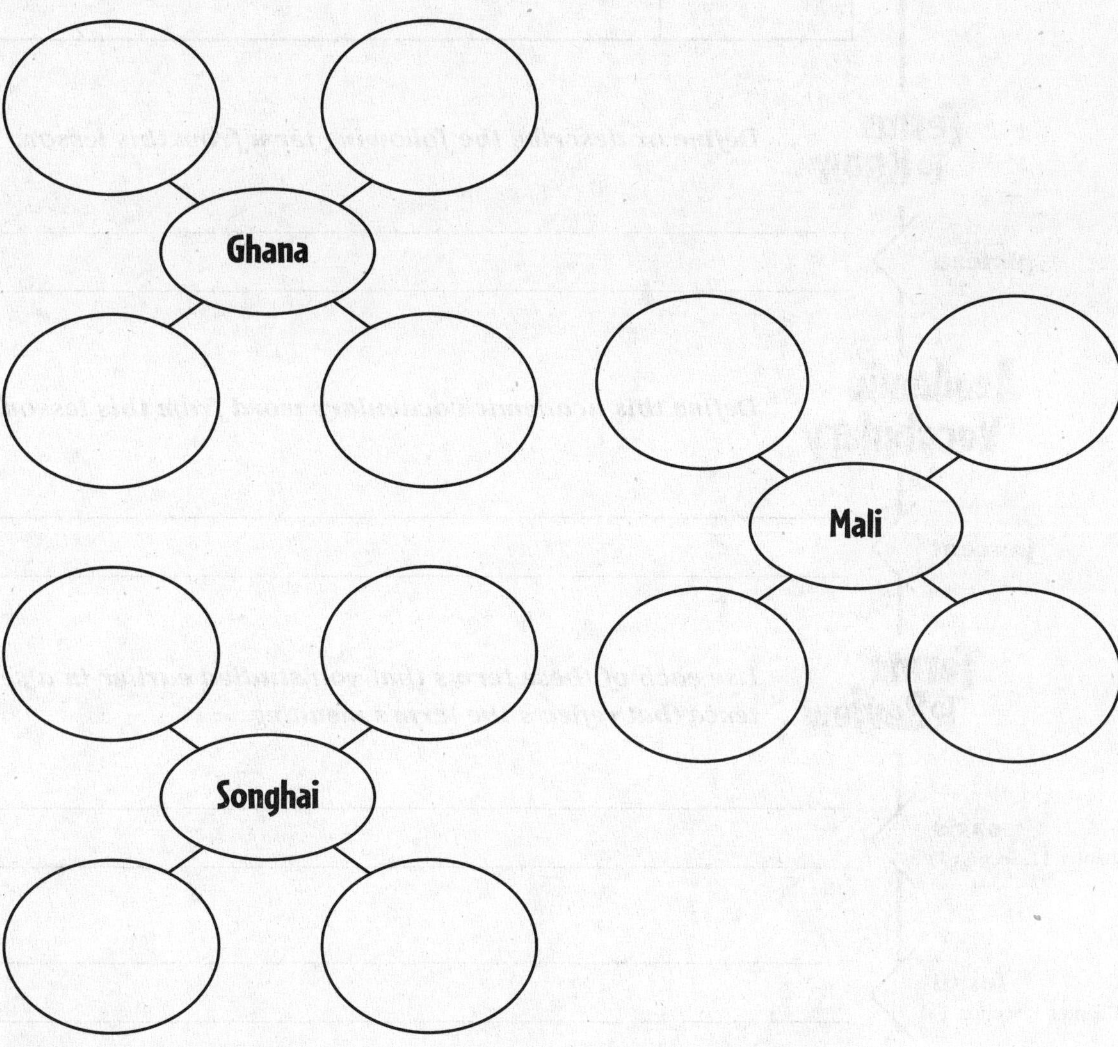

Key Points

Africa's Geography *(pages 445–446)*

Summarizing

As you read, picture yourself in the different parts of the African continent. Complete the chart below with a summary of each part of Africa. As you write, think about what it would be like to explore each of these very different places.

Tropics	
Deserts	
Plateau	

Terms To Know

Define or describe the following term from this lesson.

plateau

Academic Vocabulary

Define this academic vocabulary word from this lesson.

percent

Terms To Review

Use each of these terms that you studied earlier in a sentence that reflects the term's meaning.

oasis
(Chapter 11, Section 1)

fossil
(Chapter 1, Section 1)

Sum It Up

What caused the Great Rift Valley?

West African Empires *(pages 447–449)*

Questioning

As you read, write three questions about the main ideas presented in the text. After you have finished reading, write the answers to these questions.

1.

2.

3.

Terms To Know

Define or describe the following term from this lesson.

griot

Notes

People To Meet

Explain why these people are important.

Sundiata Keita

Mansa Musa

Sunni Ali

Places To Locate

Briefly describe the following places.

Ghana

Mali

Timbuktu

Songhai

Terms To Review

Use this term that you studied earlier in a sentence that reflects the term's meaning.

caravan
(Chapter 11, Section 1)

Sum It Up

Why did West Africa become the center of three large trade empires?

Kingdoms of the Rain Forest *(pages 450–451)*

Scanning

Before you read, scan the passage to find answers to the questions below. Then, after you read, fill in any additional information you learn.

1. What protected the kingdoms of the rain forest?

2. What crops did these kingdoms produce?

3. What items did they trade?

Sum It Up

What advantages did farmers in the rain forests have over farmers in other parts of Africa?

East Africa *(pages 451–453)*

Determining the Main Idea

As you read, identify the main idea and supporting ideas from the passage to complete the chart below.

Main Idea

Supporting Ideas

Terms To Know

Define or describe the following term from this lesson.

dhow

Places To Locate

Briefly describe the following place.

Axum

Academic Vocabulary

Define these academic vocabulary words from this lesson.

trace

impact

Sum It Up

How did new technology help East Africa's trade?

Section Wrap-up

Now that you have read the section, write the answers to the questions that were included in* Setting a Purpose for Reading *at the beginning of the lesson.

How did geography affect the development of African kingdoms?

What factors contributed to the growth of African civilizations?

Chapter 13, Section 2
Africa's Government and Religion

(Pages 460–467)

Main Idea

Setting a Purpose for Reading Think about these questions as you read:

- How did African governments develop?
- What religions and beliefs shaped life in Africa?

Reading Strategy

As you read pages 464–467 in your textbook, complete the diagram to show the components of Swahili culture and language.

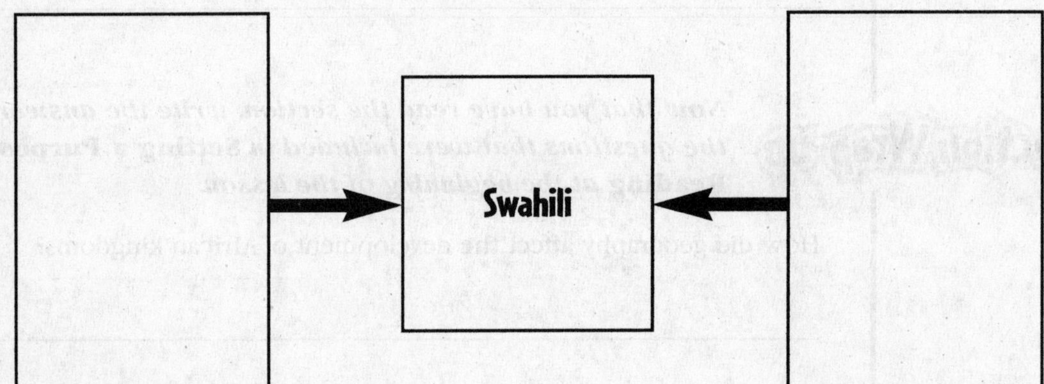

Government and Society *(pages 461–462)*

Visualizing

Imagine you are a citizen of Ghana. You have a complaint against your neighbor. You just brought your complaint before the king. Write a paragraph about your meeting with the king. What did you do? What did he do? How did you feel as you approached the king? What was happening around you?

Terms To Know

Define or describe the following term from this lesson.

clan

Academic Vocabulary

Define these academic vocabulary words from this lesson.

benefit

rely

Sum It Up

How was Mali ruled differently from Ghana?

Traditional African Religions *(page 463)*

As you read, take notes in the space below on the different African religious practices and beliefs. Then answer the question below:

African Religious Practices

Why do you think Africans held so strongly to their own religious practices?

People To Meet

Explain why this person is important.

Olaudah Equiano

Sum It Up

What was the role of ancestors in African religion?

Islam in Africa *(pages 464–467)*

Analyzing

As you read, fill in the information in the chart below. Use this chart to review information about Mansa Musa's and Askia Muhammad's role in strengthening the Islamic religion.

Growth of Islam	
Causes →	**Effects**

Terms To Know

Define or describe the following terms from this lesson.

sultan

Swahili

People To Meet

Explain why these people are important.

Ibn Battuta

Askia Muhammad

Places To Locate

Briefly describe the following place.

Makkah

Academic Vocabulary

Define these academic vocabulary words from this lesson.

survive

unique

Terms To Review

Use each of these terms that you studied earlier in a sentence that reflects the term's meaning.

Quran
(Chapter 11, Section 1)

mosque
(Chapter 11, Section 3)

Sum It Up

How did Askia Muhammad gain control of Songhai?

Now that you have read the section, write the answers to the questions that were included in* Setting a Purpose for Reading *at the beginning of the lesson.

How did African governments develop?

What religions and beliefs shaped life in Africa?

Chapter 13, Section 3
African Society and Culture

(Pages 468–476)

Main Idea

Setting a Purpose for Reading Think about these questions as you read:

- What events shaped the culture of medieval Africa?
- What effects has African culture had on other cultures around the world?

Reading Strategy

As you read pages 472–473 in your textbook, complete this Venn diagram to show the similarities and differences between the enslavement of Africans in Africa and the enslavement of Africans in Europe.

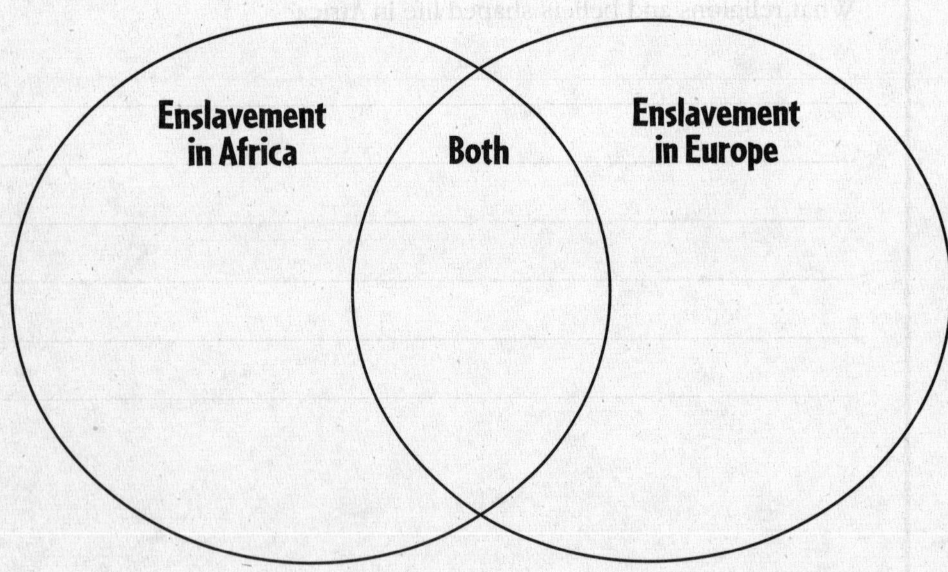

Life in Medieval Africa *(pages 469–470)*

Connecting

In West Africa, griots told stories passed down from generation to generation as part of the community's oral history. What stories have been passed down from generation to generation in your family or community? How has this story impacted you? Write the story—your oral history—and your response to it in the space below.

Terms To Know

Define or describe the following terms from this lesson.

extended family

matrilineal

oral history

People To Meet

Explain why these people are important.

Dahia al-Kahina

Nzinga

Notes

Places To Locate

Briefly describe the following place.

Benue River

Academic Vocabulary

Define these academic vocabulary words from this lesson.

generation

guarantee

Terms To Review

Use this term that you studied earlier in a sentence that reflects the term's meaning.

proverb
(Chapter 3, Section 2)

Sum It Up

How were Bantu families organized?

Slavery *(pages 472–473)*

Previewing

Preview this section to get an idea of what is ahead. First, skim the section. Then write a sentence or two explaining what you think you will be learning. After you have finished reading, revise your statements as necessary.

Academic Vocabulary

Define these academic vocabulary words from this lesson.

goal

portion

Sum It Up

How did exploration change the African slave trade?

Key Points

Notes

African Culture *(pages 474–476)*

Synthesizing

How has African culture affected your world today? As you read, note the different types of African dance, art, stories, and music in the passage. Then think about how you see African dance, art, and music in the world around you today. Write a brief paragraph about the effects of African culture in your society today.

Sum It Up

Why did Africans use dance to celebrate important events?

Section Wrap-up

Now that you have read the section, write the answers to the questions that were included in* Setting a Purpose for Reading *at the beginning of the lesson.

What events shaped the culture of medieval Africa?

What effects has African culture had on other cultures around the world?

Chapter 14, Section 1
Early Japan
(Pages 484–490)

Main Idea

Setting a Purpose for Reading Think about these questions as you read:

- How did geography affect the development of Japan?
- What ideas shaped Japan's religion and government?

Reading Strategy

As you read page 490 in your textbook, complete this diagram to show the basics of the Shinto religion.

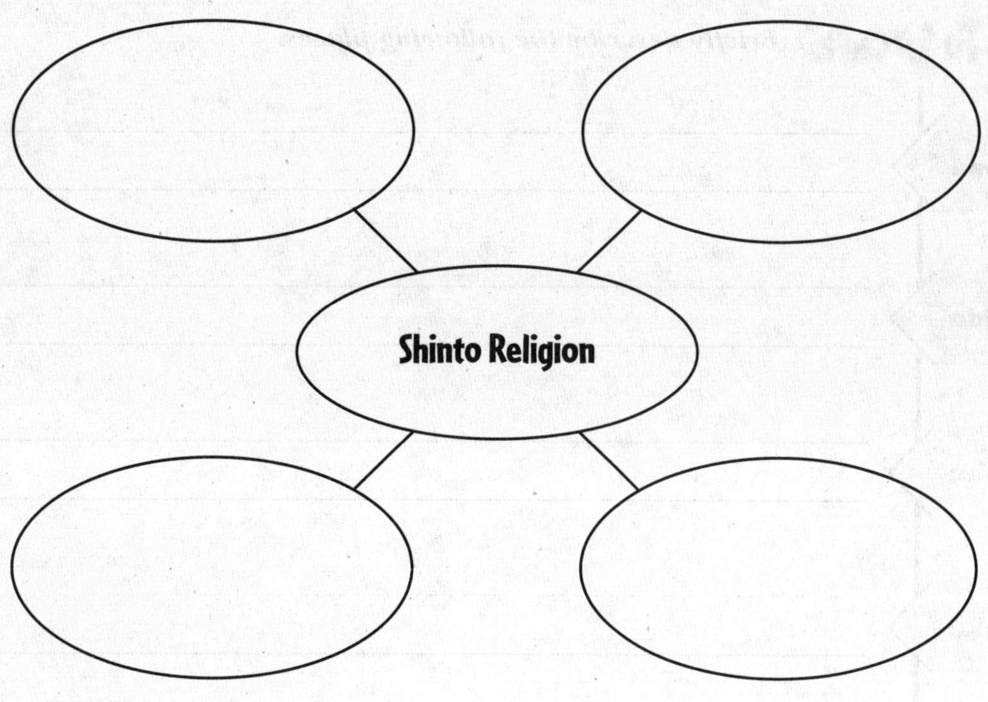

Japan's Geography *(page 485)*

Analyzing ***As you read, complete the diagram below to show the effects of geography on life in Japan.***

Cause	Effect	Effect	Effect
Mountains			
Islands			

Places To Locate ***Briefly describe the following places.***

Japan

____

____

Hokkaido

____

____

Honshu

____

____

Shikoku

____

____

Kyushu

____

____

Key Points | Notes

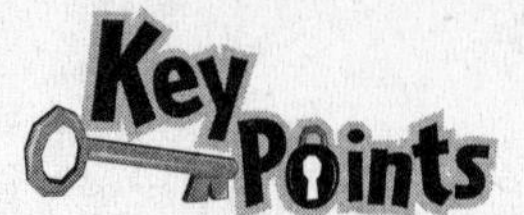

Sum It Up — ***How did Japan's geography shape its society?***

The First Settlers *(pages 486–487)*

Interpreting — ***After you read, write a brief description of each of the people, gods, and goddesses listed below. Then place names in the proper order in the diagram below to show their relationships.***

Susanowo

Amaterasu

Ninigi

Jimmu

Amaterasu → [ ] → [ ]

Terms To Know

Define or describe the following term from this lesson.

clan

People To Meet

Explain why these people are important.

Jomon

Yayoi

Terms To Review

Use this term that you studied earlier in a sentence that reflects the term's meaning.

myth
(Chapter 5, Section 1)

Sum It Up

What do historians know for sure about the rise of the Yamato?

Prince Shotoku's Reforms *(page 488)*

Determining the Main Idea

Complete the diagram below to list Prince Shotoku's reforms.

Prince Shotoku's Reforms

Terms To Know

Define or describe the following term from this lesson.

constitution

Terms To Review

Use each of these terms that you studied earlier in a sentence that reflects the term's meaning.

reform
(Chapter 12, Section 1)

monastery
(Chapter 12, Section 1)

Sum It Up

What happened during the Great Change?

What Is Shinto? *(page 490)*

Summarizing

After you read, write one or two sentences summarizing the beliefs of the Shinto religion in the space below.

Terms To Know

Define or describe the following terms from this lesson.

animism

shrine

Sum It Up

How did the Japanese honor the kami?

Now that you have read the section, write the answers to the questions that were included in* Setting a Purpose for Reading *at the beginning of the lesson.

How did geography affect the development of Japan?

What ideas shaped Japan's religion and government?

Chapter 14, Section 2
Shoguns and Samurai

(Pages 491–497)

Main Idea

Setting a Purpose for Reading Think about these questions as you read:
- How did Buddhism spread to Japan?
- Who were the shoguns and samurai?

Reading Strategy

As you read pages 493–497 in your textbook, complete the diagram to show the relationships between daimyo and samurai.

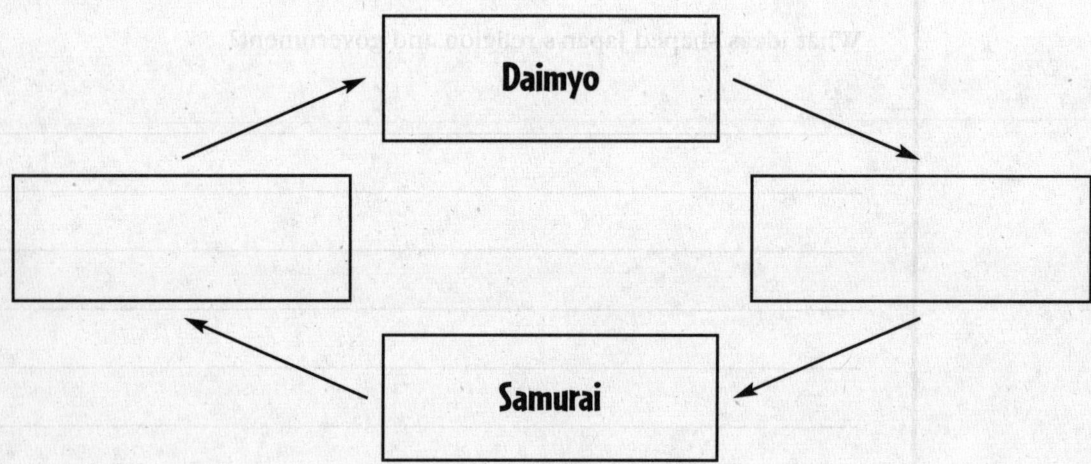

Key Points

Notes

Nara Japan *(pages 492–493)*

Inferring

After you read, answer the first two questions below. Then, use your answers to these two questions to infer the answer to the third question.

1. What did Japan's census count?

2. What were the results of the census?

3. Why was the census important in maintaining a strong central government?

Academic Vocabulary

Define this academic vocabulary word from this lesson.

estate

Terms To Review

Use this term that you studied earlier in a sentence that reflects the term's meaning.

census
(Chapter 12, Section 4)

Sum It Up

How was the Japanese system of hiring officials different from the Chinese system?

____

____

____

____

The Rise of the Shogun *(pages 493–495)*

Outlining

Complete this outline as you read.

I. The Government Weakens

A. ______________________________

B. ______________________________

C. ______________________________

II. Who Were the Samurai?

A. ______________________________

B. ______________________________

C. ______________________________

D. ______________________________

III. What Is a Shogun?

A. ______________________________

B. ______________________________

C. ______________________________

D. ______________________________

IV. The Mongols Attack

A. ______________________________

B. ______________________________

Terms To Know

Define or describe the following terms from this lesson.

samurai

shogun

People To Meet

Explain why this person is important.

Minamoto Yoritomo

Places To Locate

Briefly describe the following places.

Heian

Kamakura

Academic Vocabulary

Define these academic vocabulary words from this lesson.

enforce

design

Notes

Terms To Review

Use this term that you studied earlier in a sentence that reflects the term's meaning.

clan
(Chapter 13, Section 2)

Sum It Up

Who was the shogun, and why was he important?

The Daimyo Divide Japan *(pages 496–497)*

Predicting

Read the first paragraph on page 496. Based on your reading about Japan to this point, what do you predict will happen next? Write your prediction in the space below. Now read the entire passage. Was your prediction correct? Write your reaction to the actual events in the space provided.

Prediction

Reaction

Terms To Know

Define or describe the following terms from this lesson.

daimyo

vassal

feudalism

People To Meet

Explain why this person is important.

Ashikaga Takauji

Sum It Up

Why were shoguns unable to regain control of Japan after the Onin War?

Now that you have read the section, write the answers to the questions that were included in* Setting a Purpose for Reading *at the beginning of the lesson.

How did Buddhism spread to Japan?

Who were the shoguns and samurai?

Chapter 14, Section 3
Life in Medieval Japan

(Pages 498–504)

Main Idea

Setting a Purpose for Reading Think about these questions as you read:

- How did religion shape Japan's culture?
- What was life like for people in medieval Japan?

Reading Strategy

As you read pages 503–504 in your textbook, complete this diagram to describe the role of women in the families of medieval Japan.

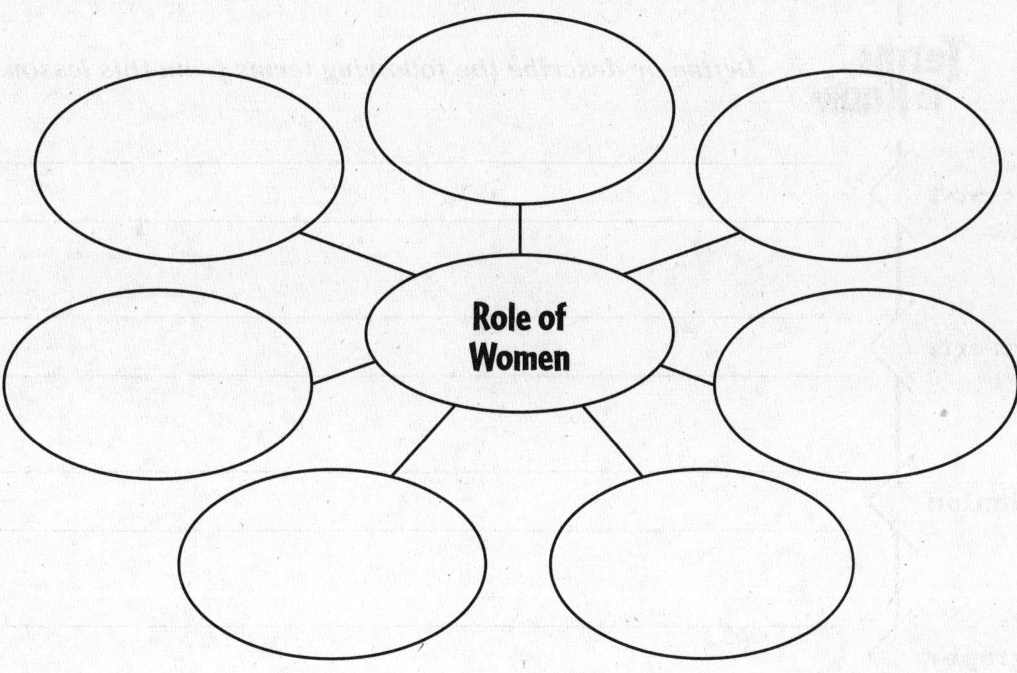

Key Points

Japanese Religion and Culture *(pages 499–501)*

Analyzing

Two sects of Buddhism were important in Japan. Use the diagram below to compare and contrast these sects. What did they have in common? How were they different?

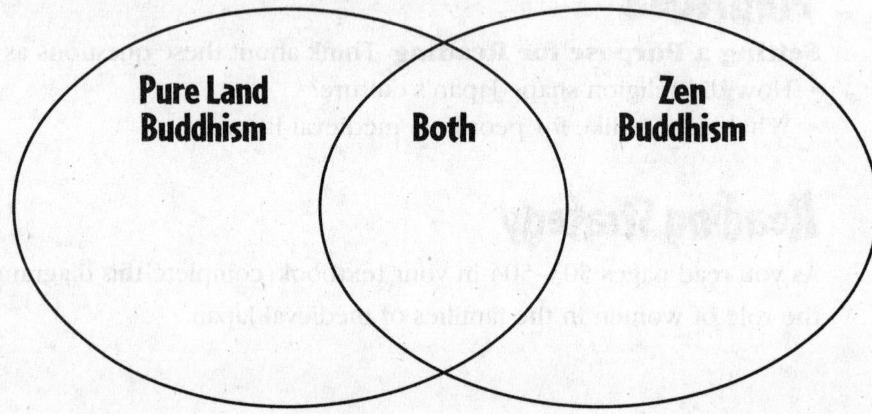

Terms To Know

Define or describe the following terms from this lesson.

sect

martial arts

meditation

calligraphy

tanka

People To Meet

Explain why this person is important.

Murasaki Shikibu

Terms To Review

Use this term that you studied earlier in a sentence that reflects the term's meaning.

novel
(Chapter 12, Section 4)

Sum It Up

How are martial arts and meditation connected to Zen Buddhism's principle of self-control?

Economy and Society *(pages 503–504)*

Previewing

Preview this section to get an idea of what is ahead. First, skim the section. Then write a sentence or two explaining what you think you will be learning. After you have finished reading, revise your statements as necessary.

Terms To Know

Define or describe the following term from this lesson.

guild

Places To Locate

Briefly describe the following place.

Kyoto

Key Points | Notes

Academic Vocabulary

Define these academic vocabulary words from this lesson.

benefit

contribute

Terms To Review

Use this term that you studied earlier in a sentence that reflects the term's meaning.

economy
(Chapter 12, Section 1)

Sum It Up

Which groups in Japan benefited from the country's wealth?

Section Wrap-up

Now that you have read the section, write the answers to the questions that were included in **Setting a Purpose for Reading** ***at the beginning of the lesson.***

How did religion shape Japan's culture?

What was life like for people in medieval Japan?

Chapter 15, Section 1
The Early Middle Ages

(Pages 512–521)

Main Idea

Setting a Purpose for Reading Think about these questions as you read:

- How did geography influence where medieval Europeans settled and what they did?
- How did religion affect life in the Middle Ages?

Reading Strategy

As you read pages 513–521 in your textbook, complete this table to show the major accomplishments of medieval leaders.

Leader	Major Accomplishments

The Geography of Europe *(pages 513–514)*

Analyzing

As you read, complete the diagram below to show the effects of geography on life in medieval Europe.

Cause	Effect	Effect
Peninsula		
Seas and rivers		
Mountains		

Academic Vocabulary

Define these academic vocabulary words from this lesson.

economy

instance

Sum It Up

What did Europe's seas and rivers provide for its people?

Key Points

Notes

The Germanic Kingdoms *(pages 514–519)*

Previewing

Look at the following headings and write a question about each one. Find answers to your questions as you read. Revise your question if the answer is not found in the reading.

The Germanic Kingdoms

Who Were the Franks?

Who Was Charlemagne?

Europe Is Invaded

The Holy Roman Empire

Terms To Know

Define or describe the following term from this lesson.

fjord

Terms To Review

Use this term that you studied earlier in a sentence that reflects the term's meaning.

legion
(Chapter 8, Section 1)

Sum It Up

Who were the Vikings, and why did they raid Europe?

The Rise of the Catholic Church *(pages 519–521)*

Summarizing

What part did each of the following people play in the rise of the Catholic Church? After you read, write one sentence about each person answering this question.

Patrick

Gregory the Great

Ethelbert

Gregory VII

Terms To Know

Define or describe the following terms from this lesson.

missionary

excommunicate

concordat

Academic Vocabulary

Define these academic vocabulary words from this lesson.

exclude

resolve

Sum It Up

How did Gregory VII and Henry IV disagree?

Now that you have read the section, write the answers to the questions that were included in* Setting a Purpose for Reading *at the beginning of the lesson.

How did geography influence where medieval Europeans settled and what they did?

How did religion affect life in the Middle Ages?

Chapter 15, Section 2

Feudalism

(Pages 522–531)

Main Idea

Setting a Purpose for Reading Think about these questions as you read:

- Why did feudalism develop in Europe?
- What was life like in a feudal society?

Reading Strategy

As you read pages 523–526 in your textbook, complete this Venn diagram to show the similarities and differences between serfs and slaves.

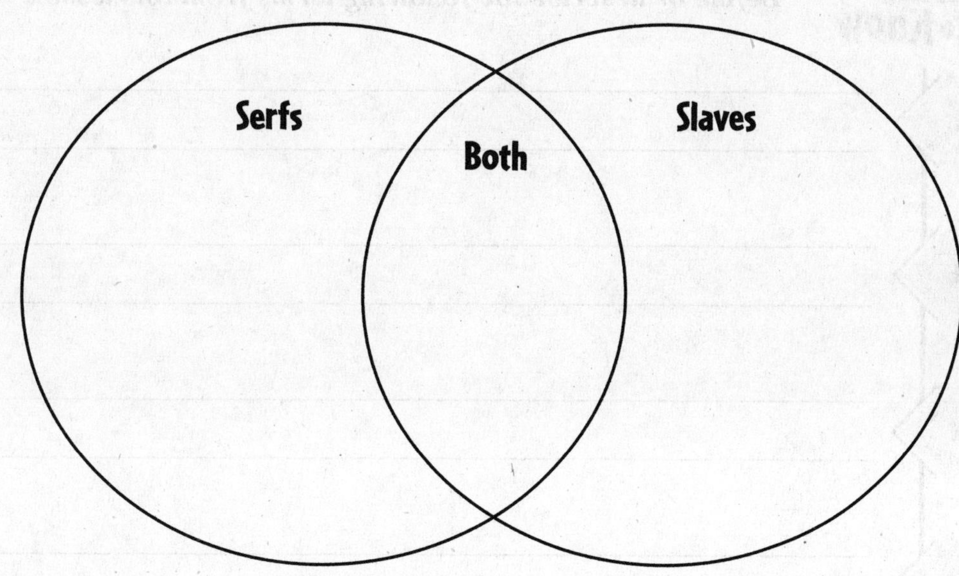

What Is Feudalism? *(pages 523–526)*

Visualizing

You live on the manor of a feudal lord in medieval Europe. Pick your role. You may be a vassal or a serf. Write an entry in your journal about the work you did today for your lord. Use details from your reading. Then add your own ideas about life in the Middle Ages.

Terms To Know

Define or describe the following terms from this lesson.

feudalism

vassal

fief

knight

serf

Academic Vocabulary

Define these academic vocabulary words from this lesson.

income

portion

Terms To Review

Use this term that you studied earlier in a sentence that reflects the term's meaning.

samurai (Chapter 14, Section 2)

Sum It Up

How could a noble be both a lord and a vassal?

Life in Feudal Europe *(pages 526–528)*

Connecting

Knights followed rules of conduct. They lived by their code of chivalry. Read about the knights' code, then write your own in the space below. Include the values that are important to you.

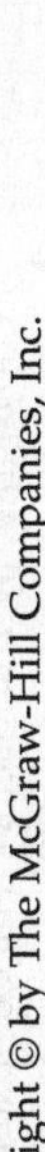

Key Points | Notes

Academic Vocabulary

Define this academic vocabulary word from this lesson.

considerable

Sum It Up

What was the code of chivalry?

Trade and Cities *(pages 528–531)*

Drawing Conclusions

Fill in the chart below to show the relationships between feudalism, new inventions, and the growth of manufacturing. Then write your answer to this question: What relationship do you see between safety and stability, technology, trade, and the economy?

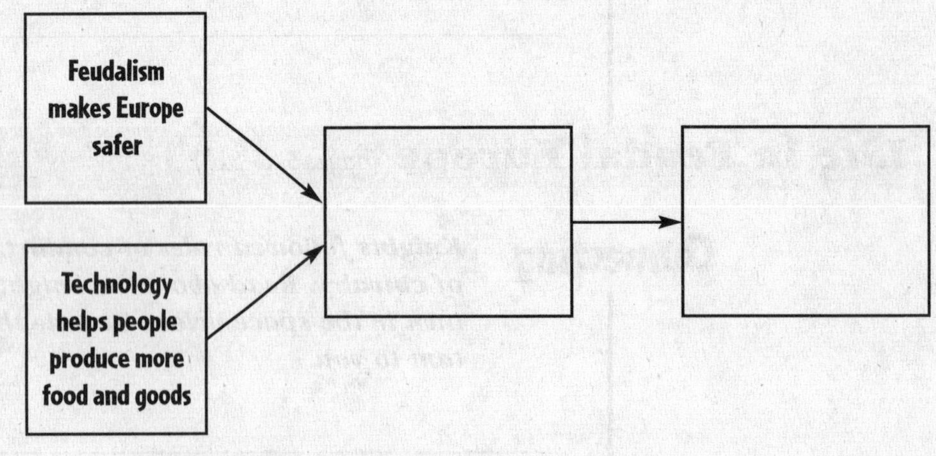

Terms To Know

Define or describe the following term from this lesson.

guild

Academic Vocabulary

Define this academic vocabulary word from this lesson.

grant

Sum It Up

In what ways do you think the shift from a barter system to a money system changed medieval Europe?

Section Wrap-up

Now that you have read the section, write the answers to the questions that were included in* Setting a Purpose for Reading *at the beginning of the lesson.

Why did feudalism develop in Europe?

What was life like in a feudal society?

Chapter 15, Section 3
Kingdoms and Crusades

(Pages 534–543)

Main Idea

Setting a Purpose for Reading Think about these questions as you read:

- What types of governments did European kingdoms create?
- Why did European Christians launch the Crusades?

Reading Strategy

As you read pages 541–543 in your textbook, complete this diagram to show the causes and effects of the Crusades.

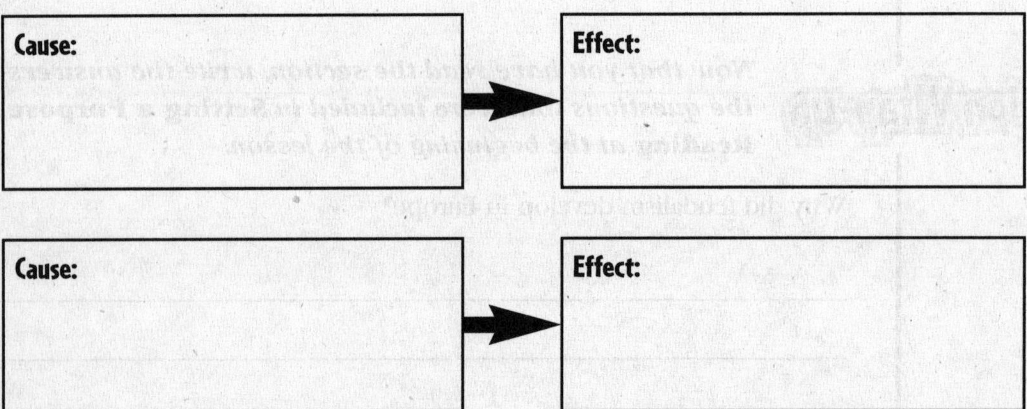

England in the Middle Ages *(pages 535–537)*

Monitoring Comprehension

As you read, answer the questions below about the Magna Carta. Review your answers to ensure you understand the document and its importance.

1. Why did the nobles force King John to sign the Magna Carta?

2. What rights were guaranteed by the Magna Carta?

3. Why is the Magna Carta important?

Terms To Know

Define or describe the following terms from this lesson.

grand jury

trial jury

Academic Vocabulary

Define these academic vocabulary words from this lesson.

region

guarantee

Sum It Up

How did the Magna Carta affect the king's power?

The Kingdom of France *(page 538)*

Evaluating

As you read, take notes on the actions of Philip IV. Then, based on your notes, write a short paragraph evaluating his leadership. Did he deserve the name Philip the Fair? Why or why not? Use specific examples from your notes to support your opinion.

Evaluation

Terms To Know

Define or describe the following term from this lesson.

clergy

Sum It Up

How did King Philip II bring power back to French kings?

Eastern Europe and Russia *(pages 539–540)*

Drawing Conclusions

Who do you think was the most important leader in Russia based on your reading? After you read, write a brief paragraph supporting your answer.

Academic Vocabulary

Define these academic vocabulary words from this lesson.

recover

version

Use this term that you studied earlier in a sentence that reflects the term's meaning.

missionary
(Chapter 10, Section 3)

____

____

Sum It Up

Why was Alexander Nevsky important?

____

____

____

The Crusades *(pages 541–543)*

Sequencing

As you read, number the following events in the correct order.

1. ____ Emperor Frederick, King Richard I, and King Philip II join to fight Saladin.

2. ____ The Crusaders create four states.

3. ____ Muslims conquer all the territory lost in the First Crusade.

4. ____ Crusaders burn and loot the Byzantine capital.

5. ____ The Muslims capture Edessa.

6. ____ The Crusaders capture Antioch and Jerusalem.

7. ____ Saladin unites the Muslims and declares war against the Christian states.

8. ____ King Richard I agrees to a truce with Saladin.

9. ____ Saladin captures Jerusalem.

Academic Vocabulary

Define these academic vocabulary words from this lesson.

aid

achieve

Sum It Up

What did the First Crusade accomplish? What did the Third Crusade accomplish?

Section Wrap-up

Now that you have read the section, write the answers to the questions that were included in* Setting a Purpose for Reading *at the beginning of the lesson.

What types of governments did European kingdoms create?

Why did European Christians launch the Crusades?

Chapter 15, Section 4
The Church and Society

(Pages 544–552)

Main Idea

Setting a Purpose for Reading Think about these questions as you read:
- What role did the Catholic Church play in medieval Europe?
- What new ideas developed in medieval Europe?

Reading Strategy

As you read pages 549–552 in your textbook, complete this Venn diagram to show the similarities and differences between Romanesque and Gothic cathedrals.

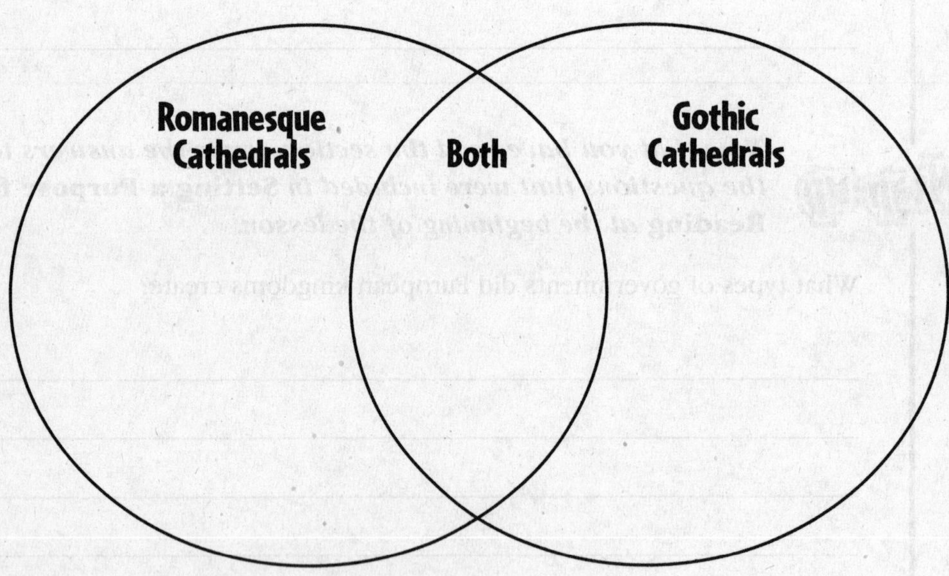

Religion and Society *(pages 545–548)*

Questioning

Before you read, scan the main headings and terms in this passage. Write four questions about the main ideas presented in the text. After you have finished reading, write the answers to these questions.

1. ______________________________

____

____

____

2. ______________________________

____

____

____

3. ______________________________

____

____

____

4. ______________________________

____

____

____

Notes

Terms To Know

Define or describe the following terms from this lesson.

mass

heresy

anti-Semitism

People To Meet

Explain why this person is important.

Francis of Assisi

Academic Vocabulary

Define these academic vocabulary words from this lesson.

conduct

enable

Sum It Up

How did the main goal of the Franciscans differ from the main goal of the Dominicans?

Medieval Culture *(pages 549–552)*

Determining the Main Idea

After you read each section, summarize the main idea of the section in one sentence in the space below.

1. Medieval Art and Architecture

2. The First Universities

3. Who Was Thomas Aquinas?

4. Medieval Literature

Terms To Know

Define or describe the following terms from this section.

theology

scholasticism

vernacular

Notes

People To Meet

Explain why this person is important.

Thomas Aquinas

Academic Vocabulary

Define these academic vocabulary words from this lesson.

logic

obtain

Terms To Review

Use each of these terms that you studied earlier in a sentence that reflects the term's meaning.

guild
(Chapter 14, Section 3)

epic
(Chapter 5, Section 1)

Sum It Up

What is natural law?

Now that you have read the section, write the answers to the questions that were included in* Setting a Purpose for Reading *at the beginning of the lesson.

What role did the Catholic Church play in medieval Europe?

____

____

____

____

____

____

What new ideas developed in medieval Europe?

____

____

____

____

____

____

Chapter 15, Section 5

The Late Middle Ages

(Pages 553–558)

Main Idea

Setting a Purpose for Reading Think about these questions as you read:

- What was the Black Death?
- What major conflicts affected life in Europe in the late Middle Ages?

Reading Strategy

As you read pages 554–555 in your textbook, complete this table to show the path of the Black Death in Europe and Asia.

Time Period	Affected Areas
1330s	
1340s	
1350s	

The Black Death *(pages 554–555)*

Inferring

After you read, write your answer to the following question in the space below.

How does a dramatic decrease in population affect the economy?

Terms To Know

Define or describe the following term from this lesson.

plague

Terms To Review

Use this term, that you studied earlier, in a sentence that reflects the term's meaning.

economy
(Chapter 12, Section 1)

Sum It Up

How many Europeans died of the plague between 1347 and 1351?

A Troubled Continent *(pages 557–558)*

Reviewing

As your read, complete the table below to summarize the conflicts in Europe in the late Middle Ages. After you read, use your table for review.

Groups in Conflict	Name of Conflict	The Cause	The Effect

Terms To Know

Define or describe the following term from this section.

Reconquista

People To Meet

Explain why each of these people is important.

Joan of Arc

Isabella of Castile

Ferdinand of Aragon

Places To Locate

Briefly describe the following places.

Crécy

Orléans

Sum It Up

What caused the Hundred Years' War?

Now that you have read the section, write the answers to the questions that were included in* Setting a Purpose for Reading *at the beginning of the lesson.

What was the Black Death?

What major conflicts affected life in Europe in the late Middle Ages?

Chapter 16, Section 1
The First Americans
(Pages 572–581)

Main Idea

Setting a Purpose for Reading Think about these questions as you read:

- Who were the first people in the Americas and how did they get there?
- What was life like for people in the first American civilizations?

Reading Strategy

As you read pages 574–581 in your textbook, complete this chart to show the characteristics of the Olmec and Moche.

	Location	Dates	Lifestyle
Olmec			
Moche			

Pathway to the Americas *(page 573)*

Analyzing ***After you read, complete the chart below to identify the effects of the end of the Ice Age.***

End of Ice Age

Terms To Know ***Define or describe the following term from this lesson.***

glacier

Academic Vocabulary ***Define these academic vocabulary words from this lesson.***

expose

estimate

Sum It Up ***Why is there no longer a land bridge between Asia and America?***

First American Civilizations *(pages 574–578)*

Drawing Conclusions

As you read, make a list of the important accomplishments of the first American civilizations. Then write a general statement that answers what these accomplishments tell you about these ancient peoples.

Civilization	Accomplishments
Olmec	
Maya	
Toltec	
Moche	
Inca	

General Statement

Terms To Know

Define or describe the following term from this lesson.

monopoly

Key Points | **Notes**

Academic Vocabulary

Define these academic vocabulary words from this lesson.

complex

resource

Terms To Review

Use each of these terms that you studied earlier in a sentence that reflects the term's meaning.

nomad (Chapter 1, Section 1)

irrigation (Chapter 1, Section 2)

Sum It Up

How did the Toltec keep other people from challenging them?

Civilizations in North America *(pages 578–581)*

Sequencing

Number the following civilizations in the order in which they appeared.

1. ____ Hopewell
2. ____ Adena
3. ____ Hohokam
4. ____ Mississippians
5. ____ Anasazi

Academic Vocabulary

Define these academic vocabulary words from this lesson.

channel

abandon

Sum It Up

How was turquoise used by the Anasazi of Chaco Canyon?

Section Wrap-up

Now that you have read the section, write the answers to the questions that were included in **Setting a Purpose for Reading** *at the beginning of the lesson.*

Who were the first people in the Americas and how did they get there?

What was life like for people in the first American civilizations?

Chapter 16, Section 2
Life in the Americas

(Pages 582–592)

Main Idea

Setting a Purpose for Reading Think about these questions as you read:

- What was life like in the Mayan, Incan, and Aztec cultures?
- How did the different climates and environments of North America shape Native American cultures?

Reading Strategy

As you read page 588 in your textbook, complete the pyramid to show Incan social classes.

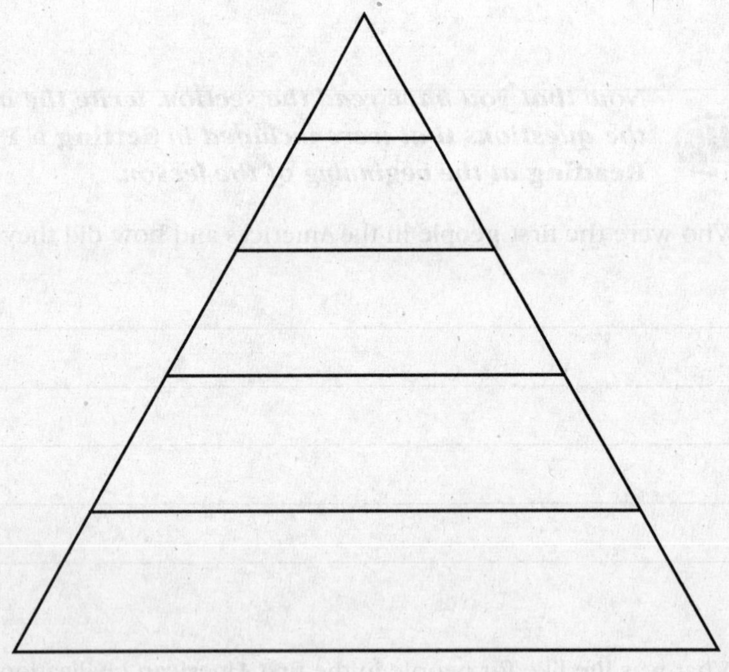

The Mayan People *(pages 583–585)*

Scanning

Glance over the reading to find details related to the following topics. After you read, fill in any missing details from the passage.

Government

Religion

Discoveries

Academic Vocabulary

Define these academic vocabulary words from this lesson.

require

predict

Key Points | Notes

Terms To Review

Use each of these terms that you studied earlier in a sentence that reflects the term's meaning.

city-state
(Chapter 1, Section 2)

____

____

hieroglyphics
(Chapter 2, Section 1)

____

____

What was the main advantage of living in a tropical rain forest?

____

____

____

____

The Aztec *(pages 585–587)*

Drawing Conclusions

As you read, look for answers to the first three questions. Then use your answers to draw a conclusion about Aztec beliefs and values. Answer this question: What do these answers tell you about the Aztec?

1. What did the Aztec expect of their kings?

____

____

____

2. Who was worthy of an afterlife and why?

____

____

____

Key Points | Notes

3. What were boys taught?

Conclusion

Terms To Review

Use this term that you studied earlier in a sentence that reflects the term's meaning.

tribute
(Chapter 2, Section 3)

Sum It Up

How could commoners move into the noble class?

Life in the Inca Empire *(page 588)*

Determining the Main Idea

As you read, summarize the contributions of Pachacuti in one sentence. Then use the chart below to list the ideas from your reading that support this main idea.

Main Idea

Supporting Ideas

Terms To Know

Define or describe the following term from this lesson.

quipu

Academic Vocabulary

Define these academic vocabulary words from this lesson.

create

ensure

Sum It Up

How did Pachacuti make sure local leaders would be loyal to him?

Life in North America *(pages 590–592)*

Reviewing

As you read, complete the table below to learn about the people who settled in North America. Use your notes for review.

Group	Climate	Food Sources	Homes
Far North			
West Coast			
Southwest			

Terms To Know

Define or describe the following terms from this lesson.

igloo

adobe

confederation

Academic Vocabulary

Define these academic vocabulary words from this lesson.

adjust

widespread

Sum It Up

How did geography shape the lives of the people north of present-day Mexico?

Section Wrap-up

Now that you have read the section, write the answers to the questions that were included in* Setting a Purpose for Reading *at the beginning of the lesson.

What was life like in the Mayan, Incan, and Aztec cultures?

How did the different climates and environments of North America shape Native American cultures?

Chapter 16, Section 3
The Fall of the Aztec and Inca Empires

(Pages 593–600)

Main Idea

Setting a Purpose for Reading Think about these questions as you read:

- How did Spain conquer Mexico?
- What brought an end to the Inca Empire?

Reading Strategy

As you read pages 595–597 in your textbook, complete this diagram to show the reasons Cortés was able to conquer the Aztec.

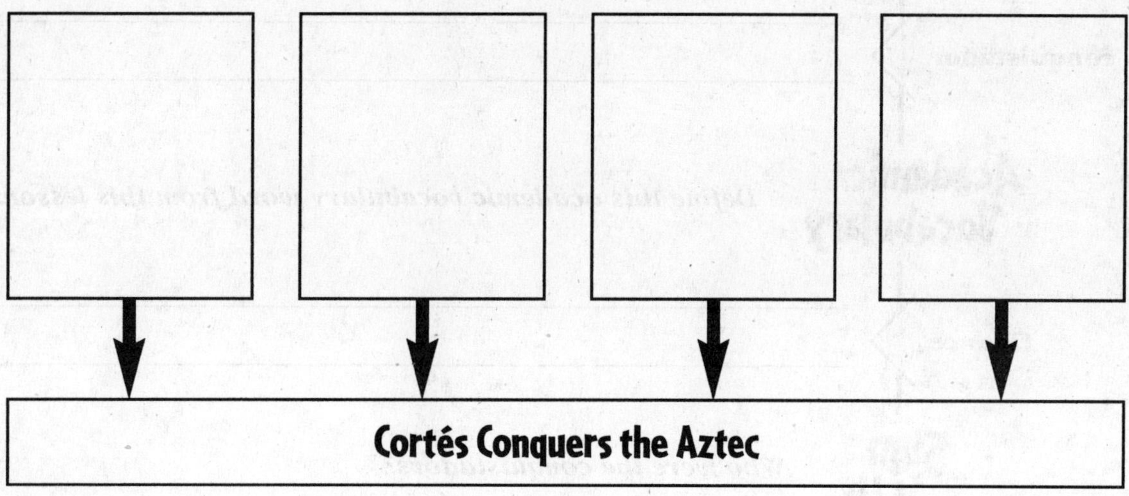

Key Points

Notes

The Spanish Arrive in America *(pages 594–595)*

Visualizing

You are one of the Taino people, living on the island of Hispaniola. For you, it is a day like any other day until you see Spanish soldier-explorers approaching from the beach. Based on the passage, write a paragraph about your first encounter with the Spaniards. How do you react to them? How do they react to you?

Terms To Know

Define or describe the following term from this lesson.

conquistador

Academic Vocabulary

Define this academic vocabulary word from this lesson.

finance

Sum It Up

Who were the conquistadors?

Spain Conquers Mexico *(pages 595–597)*

Evaluating

Did Cortés's leadership result in the defeat of the Aztec? Or did Montezuma make tactical errors? Complete the chart below to show the decisions of both Cortés and Montezuma. Then answer this question: Who played the biggest role in the defeat? Support your answer with facts from your reading.

Actions of Cortés	Actions of Montezuma

Evaluation

Academic Vocabulary

Define this academic vocabulary word from this lesson.

display

Why did the Aztec think they should welcome Cortés?

Pizarro Conquers the Inca *(pages 599–600)*

Analyzing ***After you read, answer the question below.***

Why were the Inca so easily defeated by Pizarro?

Terms To Know ***Define or describe the following term from this lesson.***

treason

Sum It Up ***How did Pizarro fail to keep his promise to Atahualpa?***

Section Wrap-up ***Now that you have read the section, write the answers to the questions that were included in* Setting a Purpose for Reading *at the beginning of the lesson.***

How did Spain conquer Mexico?

What brought an end to the Inca Empire?

Chapter 17, Section 1
The Renaissance Begins

(Pages 608–615)

Main Idea

Setting a Purpose for Reading Think about these questions as you read:

- Why did the Renaissance begin in Europe?
- How did Italy's city-states grow wealthy?

Reading Strategy

As you read pages 611–615 in your textbook, complete this chart to show the reasons Italian city-states grew wealthy.

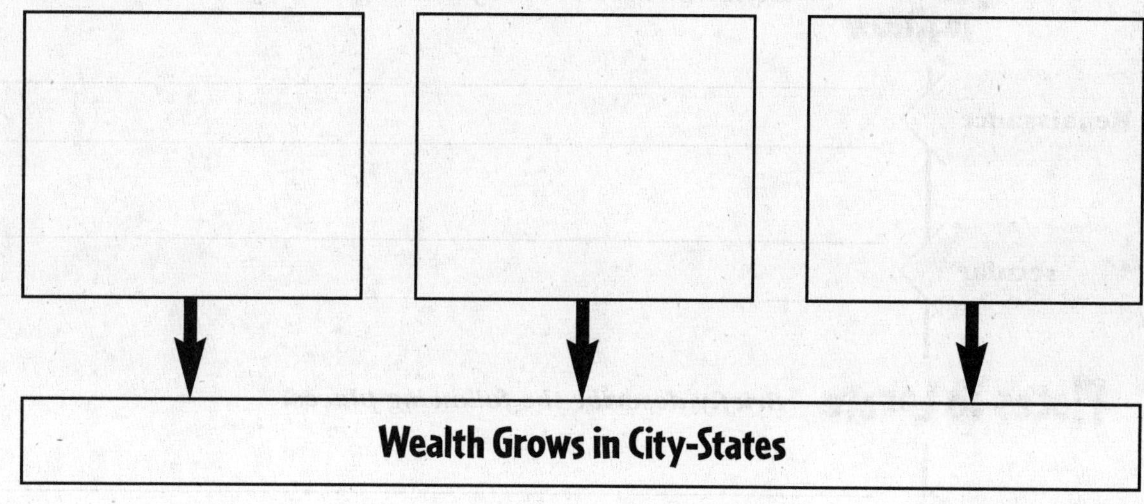

The Italian Renaissance *(pages 609–610)*

Analyzing

As you read, complete the diagram below to show the relationship between the growth of cities and the beginning of the Renaissance.

Cause	Effect/Cause	Effect
Italy's population becomes more urban	______ ______ ______	______

Terms To Know

Define or describe the following terms from this lesson.

Renaissance ______

secular ______

Places To Locate

Briefly describe the following places.

Florence ______

Venice ______

Academic Vocabulary

Define this academic vocabulary word from this lesson.

individual ______

Sum It Up *Why did the Renaissance start in Italy?*

The Rise of Italy's City-States *(pages 611–613)*

Previewing ***Before you read, look at the headings and terms in the passage. Then write four questions. Find answers to your questions as you read. Revise your questions if the answer is not found in the reading.***

1.

2.

3.

4.

People To Meet

Explain why these people are important.

Marco Polo

Medici

Academic Vocabulary

Define these academic vocabulary words from this lesson.

network

publish

Terms To Review

Use each of these terms that you studied earlier in a sentence that reflects the term's meaning.

peninsula
(Chapter 4, Section 1)

city-state
(Chapter 1, Section 2)

Sum It Up

How did Florence and the Medici family become so wealthy?

The Urban Noble *(pages 614–615)*

Responding

What is your personal response to Machiavelli's ideas about government? Do you agree or disagree? Why or why not? Present your response to Machiavelli in a brief paragraph.

Terms To Know

Define or describe the following term from this lesson.

diplomacy

Terms To Review

Use each of these terms that you studied earlier in a sentence that reflects the term's meaning.

republic
(Chapter 8, Section 1)

dictator
(Chapter 8, Section 2)

Sum It Up

How were medieval and Renaissance nobles different?

Now that you have read the section, write the answers to the questions that were included in* Setting a Purpose for Reading *at the beginning of the lesson.

Why did the Renaissance begin in Europe?

How did Italy's city-states grow wealthy?

Chapter 17, Section 2
New Ideas and Art

(Pages 618–626)

Main Idea

Setting a Purpose for Reading Think about these questions as you read:

- What is humanism and how did it affect the Renaissance?
- What makes Renaissance art different from previous art?

Reading Strategy

As you read pages 623–624 in your textbook, complete this diagram to show features of Renaissance art.

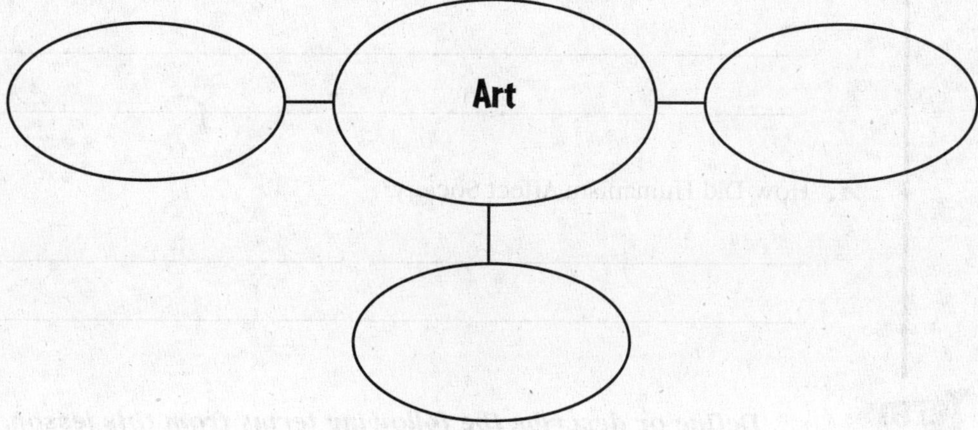

Renaissance Humanism *(pages 619–621)*

Summarizing

For each section of your reading, write a one-sentence summary of the main idea presented.

1. Ancient Works Become Popular

2. Changes in Literature

3. The Printing Press Spreads Ideas

4. How Did Humanism Affect Society?

Terms To Know

Define or describe the following terms from this lesson.

humanism

vernacular

Notes

Academic Vocabulary

Define these academic vocabulary words from this lesson.

approach

proportion

Terms To Review

Use this term that you studied earlier in a sentence that reflects the term's meaning.

fossil
(Chapter 1, Section 1)

Sum It Up

What was the benefit of writing in the vernacular?

Artists in Renaissance Italy *(pages 623–624)*

Inferring

As you read the passage, take notes about the differences between medieval and Renaissance art. Then answer this question: How was Renaissance art affected by humanism?

Key Points | Notes

Academic Vocabulary

Define these academic vocabulary words from this lesson.

fund

method

Sum It Up

What were some of the differences between medieval and Renaissance artists?

The Renaissance Spreads *(pages 625–626)*

Connecting

When have you seen a painting or picture, read a story, or seen a play or movie that made you feel a strong emotion? Why did you connect with that work of art? Write a brief paragraph describing the work of art and your reaction to it. Be sure to write about techniques used by the artist to make the work more real to you.

Academic Vocabulary

Define this academic vocabulary word from this lesson.

perspective

Terms To Review

Use each of these terms that you studied earlier in a sentence that reflects the term's meaning.

tragedy
(Chapter 5, Section 1)

comedy
(Chapter 5, Section 1)

Sum It Up

How did the Northern Renaissance differ from the Italian Renaissance?

Section Wrap-up

Now that you have read the section, write the answers to the questions that were included in* Setting a Purpose for Reading *at the beginning of the lesson.

What is humanism and how did it affect the Renaissance?

What makes Renaissance art different from previous art?

Chapter 17, Section 3
The Reformation Begins

(Pages 633–641)

Main Idea

Setting a Purpose for Reading Think about these questions as you read:

- How did Martin Luther's ideas change the Church?
- What did John Calvin teach?

Reading Strategy

As you read pages 634–637 in your textbook, complete this diagram to show the reasons for the Reformation.

Reasons for the Reformation

Calls for Church Reform *(pages 634–637)*

Outlining ***Complete this outline as you read.***

I. What Ideas Led to the Reformation?

A. ______

B. ______

II. The Church Upsets Reformers

A. ______

B. ______

C. ______

D. ______

III. Who Was Martin Luther?

A. ______

B. ______

C. ______

D. ______

E. ______

IV. Revolt Leads to New Churches

A. ______

B. ______

C. ______

V. Peasant Revolts

A. ______

B. ______

C. ______

D. ______

Terms To Know

Define or describe the following terms from this lesson.

Reformation

indulgence

denomination

Academic Vocabulary

Define these academic vocabulary words from this lesson.

challenge

thereby

Terms To Review

Use each of these terms that you studied earlier in a sentence that reflects the term's meaning.

clergy
(Chapter 10, Section 2)

salvation
(Chapter 10, Section 1)

Sum It Up

What was the result of the Church's decision to sell indulgences in 1517?

Politics and Lutheranism *(page 639)*

Synthesizing

As you read, take notes on the reasons German rulers decided to become Lutherans. Now think about different countries and governments around the world today. Some governments favor or support specific religions. Others do not. Write a paragraph summarizing your opinions about the relationship of church and government. Use specific examples from history, from current events, and from your notes to support your opinion.

Sum It Up

Why did many German princes support Martin Luther's ideas?

Calvin and Calvinism *(pages 640–641)*

Scanning

Glance quickly over the reading to find answers to the following questions.

1. Who was John Calvin?

2. What is Calvinism?

Terms To Know

Define or describe the following terms from this lesson.

theology

predestination

Academic Vocabulary

Define these academic vocabulary words from this lesson.

debate

convince

Sum It Up

How did Calvin's ideas differ from those of Luther?

Section Wrap-up

Now that you have read the section, write the answers to the questions that were included in* Setting a Purpose for Reading *at the beginning of the lesson.

How did Martin Luther's ideas change the Church?

What did John Calvin teach?

Chapter 17, Section 4
Catholics and Protestants

(Pages 642–650)

Main Idea

Setting a Purpose for Reading Think about these questions as you read:
- What was the Counter-Reformation?
- What were the results of the Reformation in England?

Reading Strategy

As you read pages 643–646 in your textbook, complete this diagram to show the results of the Catholic Church's attempts to reform.

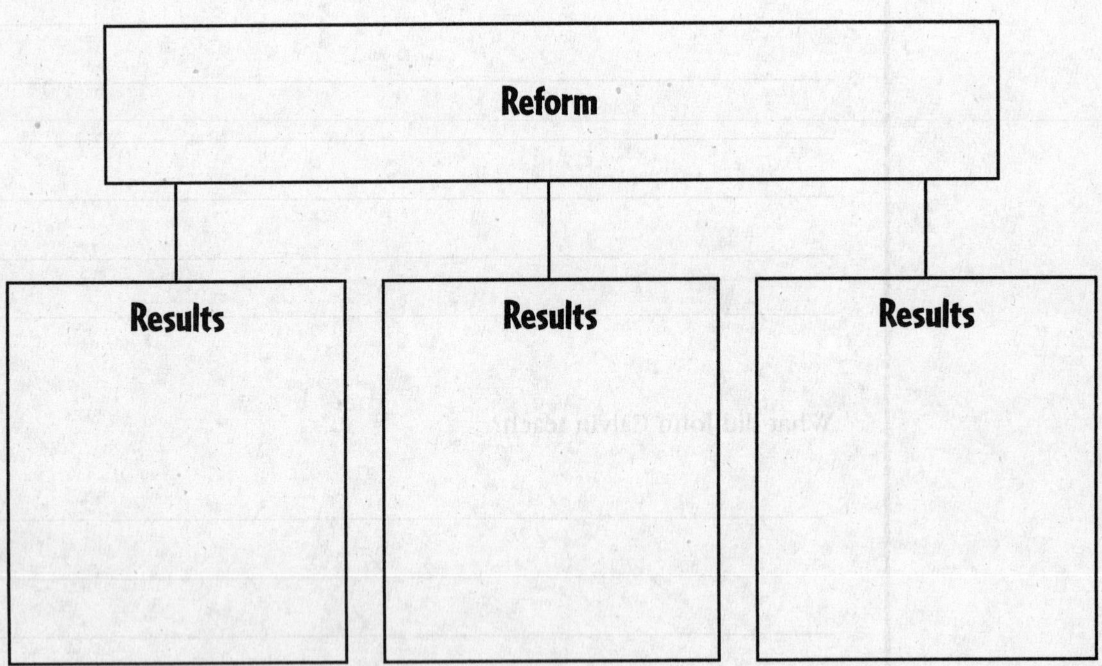

Counter-Reformation *(pages 643–646)*

Monitoring Comprehension

As you read, list the effects of the Reformation on the following kingdoms in the chart below.

France	
Bohemia	
Spain	

Terms To Know

Define or describe the following terms from this lesson.

seminary ____________________

heresy ____________________

People To Meet

Explain why each of these people is important.

Ignatius of Loyola ____________________

Henry of Navarre ____________________

Places To Locate

Briefly describe the following places.

Trent ____________________

Navarre

Paris

Academic Vocabulary

Define these academic vocabulary words from this lesson.

contradict

convert

Terms To Review

Use each of these terms that you studied earlier in a sentence that reflects the term's meaning.

reform
(Chapter 9, Section 2)

pope
(Chapter 10, Section 2)

Sum It Up

What deal earned Henry of Navarre the French throne?

The English Reformation *(pages 648–649)*

Predicting

Think about what you have already read about the effects of the Reformation in Spain, France, and the Roman Empire. Now, before you read, make a prediction about what will happen in England. After you read, write your response to the actual events.

Prediction

Reaction

Terms To Know

Define or describe the following term from this section.

annul

Places To Locate

Briefly describe the following place.

London

People To Meet

Explain why each of these people is important.

Henry VIII

Key Points | **Notes**

Mary I

Elizabeth I

Terms To Review

Use this term that you studied earlier in a sentence that reflects the term's meaning.

excommunicate
(Chapter 10, Section 3)

Sum It Up

Why did Henry VIII create the Anglican Church?

Missionaries Go Overseas *(page 650)*

Determining the Main Idea

As you read, write the main idea of the passage. Review your statement when you have finished reading and revise as needed.

Academic Vocabulary

Define this academic vocabulary word from this lesson.

overseas

Terms To Review

Use each of these terms that you studied earlier in a sentence that reflects the term's meaning.

shogun
(Chapter 14, Section 2)

missionary
(Chapter 10, Section 3)

Sum It Up

In what parts of the world did Catholic missionaries teach?

Now that you have read the section, write the answers to the questions that were included in* Setting a Purpose for Reading *at the beginning of the lesson.

What was the Counter-Reformation?

What were the results of the Reformation in England?

Chapter 18, Section 1
The Age of Exploration
(Pages 658–669)

Main Idea

Setting a Purpose for Reading Think about these questions as you read:

- Where did the Europeans explore and what did they do there?
- What were the results of global exploration?

Reading Strategy

As you read pages 659–660 in your textbook, complete this diagram to show why Europeans began to explore.

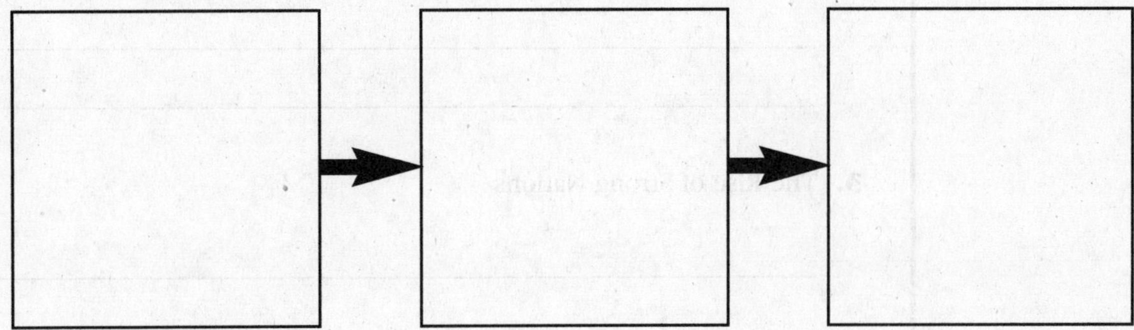

Key Points

Notes

Europe Gets Ready to Explore *(pages 659–660)*

Summarizing

How did the events listed in this passage lead to exploration? As you read, write a one-sentence summary for each of the main headings to answer this question.

1. Trade With Asia

2. New Technology

3. The Rise of Strong Nations

4. Did Maps Encourage Exploration?

Academic Vocabulary

Define this academic vocabulary word from this lesson.

technology

Sum It Up ***What were the main reasons the Europeans began exploring the world in the 1400s?***

Exploring the World *(pages 661–664)*

Questioning ***Before you read, look at the headings and terms in the passage. Then write four questions. Find answers to your questions as you read. Revise your questions if the answer is not found in the reading.***

1.

2.

3.

4.

Notes

Places To Locate

Briefly describe the following place.

Strait of Magellan

People To Meet

Explain why these people are important.

Vasco da Gama

Christopher Columbus

Ferdinand Magellan

John Cabot

Jacques Cartier

Academic Vocabulary

Define these academic vocabulary words from this lesson.

research

license

Sum It Up

Who was the first European to sail to India? Whose crew was first to sail around the world?

The Commercial Revolution *(pages 666–667)*

Analyzing

How did exploration affect European economies? After you read, complete the diagram below to analyze the effects of exploration on trade and commerce.

Effects

Cause: European exploration

Terms To Know

Define or describe the following terms from this lesson.

mercantilism

export

import

colony

Key Points | Notes

commerce

invest

Places To Locate ***Briefly describe the following place.***

Moluccas

Sum It Up ***How did merchants raise the money for overseas trade?***

A Global Exchange *(pages 668–669)*

Evaluating ***What were the positive and negative effects of the Columbian Exchange? After you read, complete the chart below to evaluate the costs and benefits of a global exchange.***

Positive Effects	Negative Effects

Terms To Review

Use these terms that you studied earlier in a sentence that reflects the term's meaning.

shogun
(Chapter 14, Section 2)

daimyo
(Chapter 14, Section 2)

Sum It Up

Describe the Columbian Exchange.

Section Wrap-up

Now that you have read the section, write the answers to the questions that were included in* Setting a Purpose for Reading *at the beginning of the lesson.

Where did the Europeans explore and what did they do there?

What were the results of global exploration?

Chapter 18, Section 2
The Scientific Revolution

(Pages 670–679)

Main Idea

Setting a Purpose for Reading Think about these questions as you read:

- How did the Scientific Revolution change life in the 1600s?
- What is the scientific method and how did it change ideas about society?

Reading Strategy

As you read pages 671–675 in your textbook, complete this diagram to show the similarities and differences in the views of Ptolemy and Copernicus.

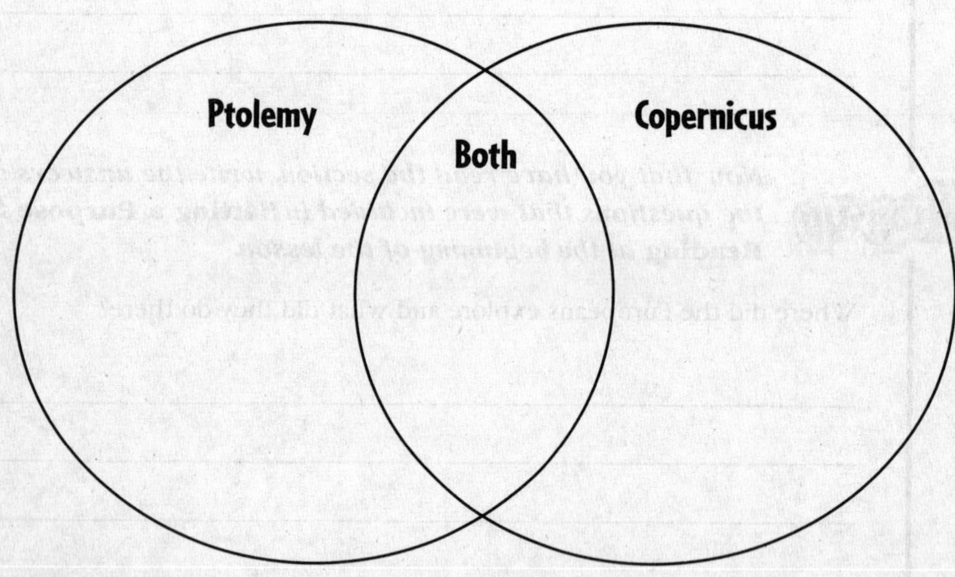

The Scientific Revolution *(pages 671–673)*

Monitoring Comprehension

What factors led to the growth of scientific knowledge in Europe? As you read, list the factors in the chart below.

Scientific Knowledge Grows in Europe

Terms To Know

Define or describe the following term from this lesson.

theory

Terms To Review

Use each of these terms that you studied earlier in a sentence that reflects the term's meaning.

acupuncture
(Chapter 7, Section 3)

theology
(Chapter 17, Section 3)

Sum It Up

Describe scientific knowledge during the Middle Ages.

Key Points

Notes

A Revolution in Astronomy *(pages 673–675)*

Inferring

As you read the passage, take notes on Galileo's experiments. Think about what you have read so far about the Catholic Church. Then answer this question: Why did the Catholic Church force Galileo to withdraw many of his statements?

People To Meet

Explain why this person is important.

Kepler

Academic Vocabulary

Define this academic vocabulary word from this lesson.

revolution

Terms To Review

Use each of these terms that you studied earlier in a sentence that reflects the term's meaning.

pope
(Chapter 10, Section 2)

heresy
(Chapter 17, Section 4)

Sum It Up

How did Galileo prove Copernicus's theory?

New Scientific Discoveries *(pages 675–676)*

Reviewing

As you read, complete the chart below to identify the major discoveries in the Scientific Revolution. Use your notes to review later.

Scientist	Discovery

Notes

Academic Vocabulary

Define these academic vocabulary words from this lesson.

element

contribute

Sum It Up

According to Newton, what force held the planets in orbit?

The Triumph of Reason *(pages 678–679)*

Sequencing

Write the steps of the scientific method in the proper order in the diagram below.

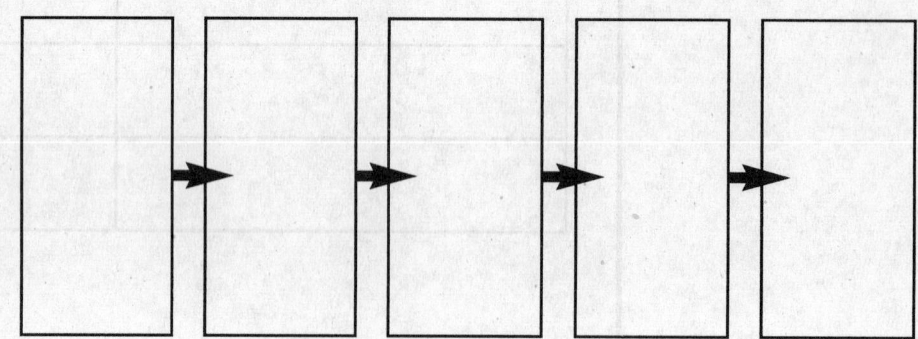

Terms To Know

Define or describe the following terms from this lesson.

rationalism

scientific method

hypothesis

People To Meet

Explain why this person is important.

Descartes

Academic Vocabulary

Define these academic vocabulary words from this lesson.

obvious

principle

Sum It Up

What is the scientific method?

Now that you have read the section, write the answers to the questions that were included in* Setting a Purpose for Reading *at the beginning of the lesson.

How did the Scientific Revolution change life in the 1600s?

What is the scientific method and how did it change ideas about society?

Chapter 18, Section 3
The Enlightenment
(Pages 680–689)

Main Idea

Setting a Purpose for Reading Think about these questions as you read:
- What was the Enlightenment?
- How did Enlightenment ideas affect government?

Reading Strategy

As you read pages 681–689 in your textbook, complete this table to show the major ideas of Enlightenment thinkers.

Thinkers	Ideas

New Ideas About Politics *(pages 681–682)*

Analyzing

As you read, complete the Venn diagram below to compare and contrast the views of Hobbes and Locke on government.

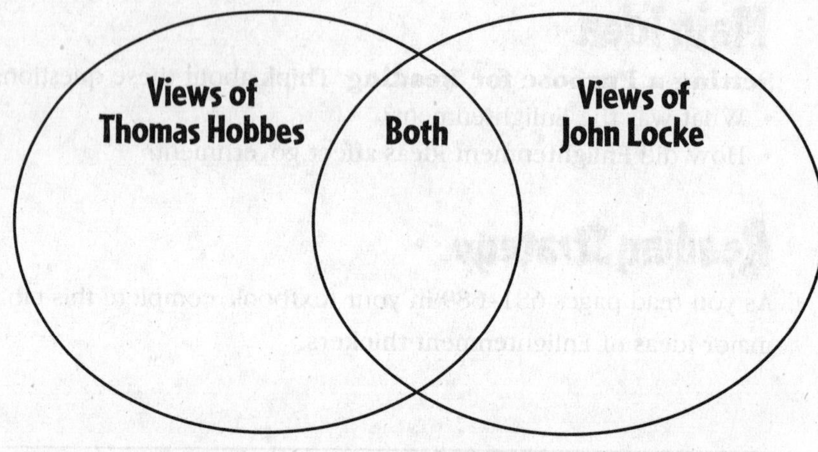

Terms To Know

Define or describe the following terms from this lesson.

natural law

social contract

separation of powers

People To Meet

Explain why this person is important.

Montesquieu

Notes

Academic Vocabulary

Define these academic vocabulary words from this lesson.

reveal

contract

Sum It Up

According to Montesquieu, how should government be organized?

The French Philosophes *(pages 684–686)*

Evaluating

Select one of the philosophers from your reading and evaluate his or her ideas. Do you agree with the ideas? Do you disagree? Write a brief paragraph summarizing your view of the philosopher's ideas.

Terms To Know

Define or describe the following term from this lesson.

deism

People To Meet

Explain why this person is important.

Voltaire

Academic Vocabulary

Define these academic vocabulary words from this lesson.

maintain

range

Sum It Up

Who were the philosophes?

The Age of Absolutism *(pages 686–689)*

Skimming

Quickly look over the entire selection to get a general idea about the reading. Then briefly describe what the selection is about on the lines below.

Notes

Terms To Know

Define or describe the following term from this lesson.

absolutism

Places To Locate

Briefly describe the following places.

Prussia

Austria

St. Petersburg

Terms To Review

Use this term that you studied earlier in a sentence that reflects the term's meaning.

serf
(Chapter 15, Section 2)

Sum It Up

How did the ideas of absolute monarchs conflict with the ideas of Enlightenment thinkers?

Now that you have read the section, write the answers to the questions that were included in* Setting a Purpose for Reading *at the beginning of the lesson.

What was the Enlightenment?

How did Enlightenment ideas affect government?

Chapter 18, Section 4
The American Revolution
(Pages 690–700)

Main Idea

Setting a Purpose for Reading Think about these questions as you read:

- What ideas of government influenced Americans?
- Why did American colonists fight to form a new nation?

Reading Strategy

As you read pages 695–698 in your textbook, complete this cause-and-effect diagram to show why the British colonies declared independence.

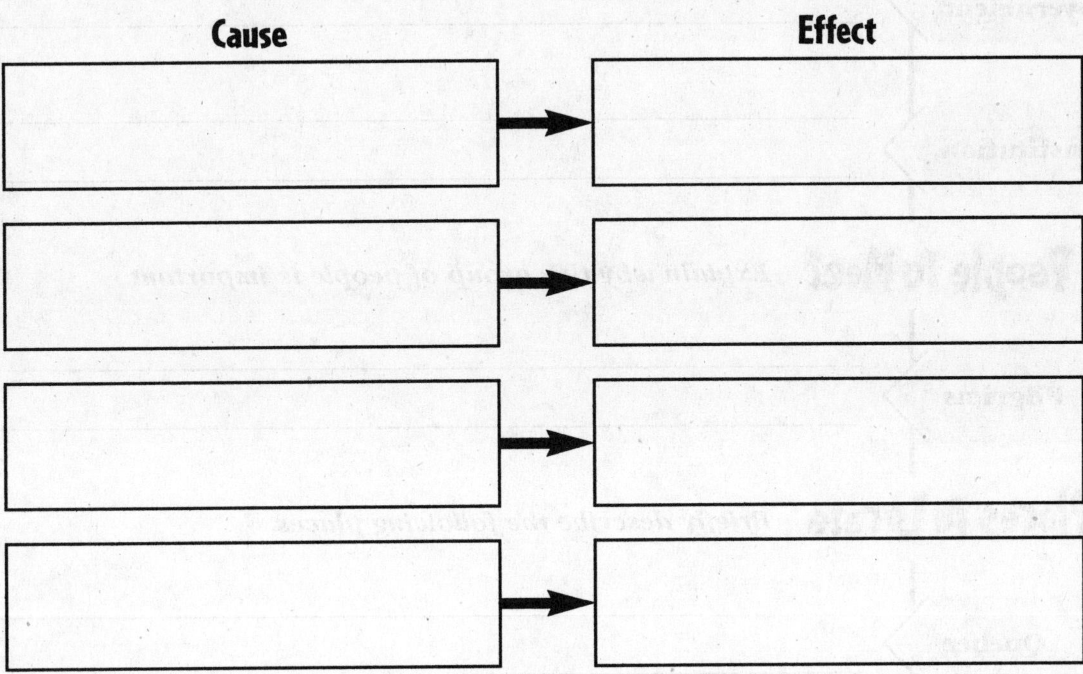

Key Points Notes

Settling North America *(pages 691–694)*

Monitoring Comprehension

As you read, complete the diagram below to identify the reasons that English settlers came to North America.

Reasons English Settlers Came to America

Terms To Know

Define or describe the following terms from this lesson.

representative government

constitution

People To Meet

Explain why this group of people is important.

Pilgrims

Places To Locate

Briefly describe the following places.

Quebec

Jamestown

Terms To Review

Use this term that you studied earlier in a sentence that reflects the term's meaning.

conquistador
(Chapter 16, Section 3)

Sum It Up

How was the funding of Jamestown different from the funding of Plymouth?

____

____

____

____

Trouble in the Colonies *(pages 695–698)*

Sequencing

What events led to the American Revolution? Number the events below to show the order in which they occurred.

1. ____ Parliament passes the Stamp Act

2. ____ Violence breaks out at the Boston Massacre

3. ____ The British defeat the French and gain nearly all of their North American empire

4. ____ Parliament passes the Tea Act

5. ____ Parliament closes Boston Harbor and passes the Intolerable Acts

6. ____ Delegates from the 12 colonies meet in Philadelphia

7. ____ Angry colonists toss English tea into Boston Harbor

8. ____ Britain passes the Navigation Acts

Places To Locate

Briefly describe the following place.

Boston

____

____

Key Points | Notes

Academic Vocabulary

Define these academic vocabulary words from this lesson.

impose

guarantee

Terms To Review

Use this term that you studied earlier in a sentence that reflects the term's meaning.

veto
(Chapter 8, Section 2)

Sum It Up

What was the Boston Tea Party?

The War of Independence *(pages 698–700)*

What ideas influenced American ideas about government and independence? And where did these ideas come from? As you read, complete the chart below to answer these questions.

Source	Ideas

Notes

Terms To Know

Define or describe the following terms from this lesson.

popular sovereignty

limited government

People To Meet

Explain why each of these people is important.

George Washington

Tom Paine

Thomas Jefferson

Places To Locate

Briefly describe the following place.

Philadelphia

Terms To Review

Use this term that you studied earlier in a sentence that reflects the term's meaning.

republic
(Chapter 8, Section 1)

Notes

Sum It Up

Why did the colonists decide to separate from Great Britain to create a new nation?

Section Wrap-up

Now that you have read the section, write the answers to the questions that were included in* Setting a Purpose for Reading *at the beginning of the lesson.

What ideas of government influenced Americans?

Why did American colonists fight to form a new nation?